THE ART
OF
FLIRTING

The Art of Flirting ™

Published by Dating Boutique LLC

www.datingboutiqueinc.com

Front Cover designed by Amanda Rose

This book is dedicated to my children who inspire
me everyday to achieve my dreams and help create
better relationships in this world.

TABLE OF CONTENTS

ABOUT

Hi, I'm Amanda Rose. I'm a celebrity matchmaker and dating expert. I've been in the industry since 2012 and have multiple businesses in the dating industry. I'm the Founder of the Dating Stylist, the Dating Boutique, Prestige Connections, and SwoonMe Events. I was recently named Top Celebrity Matchmaker of the Year, Top Dating Coach of the Year, Best Matchmaker of Savannah, Best Dating Service of Charlotte and listed as one of the top women leaders of North Carolina. The mission of all my companies is to help singles heal from past relationships, enjoy the journey of being single, and ultimately to help them find "the one."

I started my journey in the dating industry in 2012 by accident. I was married at the time and had suspicions my husband was dating online. So, I did what any suspicious wife would do... I went looking for his online dating profile. As I was searching for his profile I thought to myself, *Wow, how are these guys getting dates?! The profiles look horrible. There should be a business that helps people look dateable!* Shortly after that thought crossed my mind I came upon my then husband. I found his profile full of photos that I took on family vacations, his "single" status, and his fake area code. Needless to say we got a divorce.

The divorce was emotionally and physically devastating. I went from being a stay-at-home mom to a single mom overnight. However, after one day of crying on my bedroom floor, something came over me. I knew I had two choices in that moment. #1) I could let this divorce destroy me or #2) I could pick myself up and create the life of my dreams for me and my children.

I chose option two.

As we were going through the divorce, I thought, *I should start that business*. A business giving makeovers to online dating profiles to help them look dateable and help singles date better.

However, I knew I was the common denominator in my failed marriage and any relationships before. I knew I had some deep healing to do when it came to relationships before I helped other singles. So, I got to work. I started teaching myself how to create a business, I studied the dating industry until the late hours, and I went back to college to study intimate communication.

There was one point when I worked four jobs while also working on the new business just to survive. I had two little kids to take care of, but I had a huge vision of what I could create.

Early on in my business I received a call from a producer with the Steve Harvey Show. I thought it was a bad joke my ex-husband was playing on me. But it wasn't. The producer wanted me to come on the show and makeover singles' online dating profiles. I didn't even have a client yet! I scrambled to come up with some before/after examples for the producer. I enlisted a co-founder to help me get the business off and running and to help produce the content needed. I was inexperienced and picked the wrong co-founder. The co-founder never got the content to the producer like they promised and the opportunity passed us by. However, it was in that moment I knew I had something and continued to build the business over the years.

Since then I have built three additional businesses, I've been named one of the top dating coaches in the world,the top celebrity match-maker, I've worked with celebrities and billionaires, and I have been featured on numerous media including *Glamour, TIme, Redbook, Great Day Live*, the *TD Jakes Show, Forbes, Martha Stewart*, and more.

I've poured a lot of what I have learned over the years about flirting, dating, and communication into this book. I couldn't fit all my matchmaking secrets in, but I promise there will be more to come.

I hope you enjoy the actionable and relatable steps I've included in this book, which was inspired by my best selling course "The Art of Flirting." If you want more, dive even deeper into the art of flirting and check out the course to go along with this content.

My goal was to keep the book simple, relatable, and actionable. Because you won't attract Mr. Right sitting at home, I fully expect you to take what you learn and put it into action. My dream for this book is that it will give you more confidence to attract "the one" with authenticity and ease, while enjoying your journey along the way.

XO,

Amanda Rose

INTRODUCTION

Welcome. I am so excited that you're here! I can't wait for you to get started on this journey of flirting and becoming the irresistible woman that you are. This is so much more than just reading a book about flirting, this is a book to love on you, to show you how incredibly worthy and loved you are, and to put all of that into action to find "the one" with confidence and ease. Often, people forget that beautiful, authentic flirting is more about bringing out the best version of yourself, engaging with a new person, making a beautiful lasting connection, and making it fun of course! The truth is, flirting doesn't stop at dating. Flirting is something we carry on into our relationship to make it fun, exciting, and playful. Just imagine ten or twenty years from now and you are still flirting with your spouse. How fun will that be? That's the stuff to get excited about. So, you can take what you learn today and carry it on to that perfect person that you end up with forever.

I can't wait to dig in and get started! There will be actionable tips that you can practice on your own and take out into this world. I do not intend for the actionable tips to stop just at this book. The goal of this book is to ensure everything taught is learned and put into action. I want you to make real life connections, to increase your self-confidence, and walk into a room and shine. I know you can, I know you are created with beauty and grace. So you need to own it and I'm certain you will because I believe in you. I know you're going to get out there, put all you've learned into action, and have fun along the journey.

Before I created this book, I taught hundreds of clients how to actually get out there, flirt, and make connections. I took them out with me, and we found people for them to approach. It was hands on—get out there and do this thing. It was so much fun, and it's often a huge step for someone because it can be scary to approach someone you don't know and start a conversation. Let alone trying to flirt with them.

Flirting and making new connections can take us out of our comfort zone, especially if it is not natural to us. However, getting out of your comfort zone is a good thing. Often, the best things in life are on the other side of fear, or on the other side of our comfort zone. When I asked my clients what I should tell everyone in this book, they all basically said the same thing: "It works if you work it." With that in mind, this isn't a book that you can just read then set aside and expect miracles to happen.

Miracles are definitely possible, and they happen all the time with my clients—there's something magical about being a matchmaker—however, you have to take action and work on the principles, you have to take inspired actions to get the results you want. That's a non-negotiable.

So, stay in your pajamas at home, grab some coffee, tea, or a glass of wine, and enjoy the book. But after that, I want you to get out there and work it. You can't stay behind the computer screen, if you don't do the work behind this book, it's certainly not going to work for you. You're not going to find Mr. or Miss Right from home. Not once has a perfect partner dropped from the sky while someone was at home watching Netflix. So, you have to get out there, do the work every single week. Do the homework in each chapter because that's where all the magic happens. It happens when you do the homework, you take it out there and take action on what you've learned. I'll give you prompts on what to do for those steps. You have this book for life, so go back and practice them as needed. Practice always makes perfect! Show up every single day to accomplish your goals.

Now, I didn't learn all this dating expert stuff overnight. It actually took me years of studying and putting it into action, and I'm putting it all into a book for you to learn at a faster pace, to get out there and make things happen for you much faster than it did for me.

I look forward to feedback on how it goes. If you have any questions during your read, feel free to reach out to our support team at info@datingboutiqueinc.com. We would love to hear how it goes for you. For more resources on all things love and dating visit www.datingboutiqueinc.com.

Let's get started and dig into chapter one.

DATING WITH INTENTION

I'm so excited to get this book out into the world! I want you to be successful, and I want you to fully understand the foundation of relationship excellence. I want you to understand the foundation of setting yourself up for success and what that means in the dating world and relationships. When you go through any book, program, or you have any goal when you're dating, you need to have this foundation. I talk about this a lot in my trainings. I can't leave this part out because it's vital in the process of mastering relationships and authentic connections.

In chapter one, we're going to set the foundation for you to be successful in dating and relationships. You'll take the foundations of success to the future relationship with your partner. This journey is designed to create amazing, healthy, lifelong relationships. As a matchmaker, my goal isn't just for you to date successfully, I want you to get from point A to point B, find your soulmate, and be in a healthy relationship forever. My ultimate goal is for you to create that amazing relationship that you've desired for so long. I intend to teach you how to date successfully, how to find that person, and then how to keep that healthy relationship going. All of this put together is what's amazing about this book. The Art of Flirting is a great resource right now when you're single and looking for your soulmate. But the cool thing is; you can take this into your relationship with your future husband, because flirting doesn't stop after the dating stage. The truth is—you should never stop flirting with your partner. Your partner is there to have a lifelong experience of passion, friendship, and fun.

Okay, let's get started. One thing that I like to talk about when I'm working with my clients is limiting beliefs. A lot of times my clients have limiting beliefs around relationships and dating. The first step that we are going to process together is how to shift your mindset to be successful when you're making new connections and flirting. You can't have a mind full of limiting beliefs when you're out there looking for love.

Chapter one is about the science behind flirting and how it is uniquely ingrained in everyone. It's really interesting how you can use your personality style to flirt, to gain the attention of someone, to spark those conversations, and to get someone interested. However, there's a foundation that we need to cover to set you up for success. A foundation of creating the self-confidence to flirt and to cover anything that may be holding you back mentally or emotionally. We want to cover those things so that we can overcome them and push you along the path to success.

First, I want to cover some groundwork, so grab a journal and take notes. The intention is that you dig deep into this portion of the book, which will eventually help you set that strong foundation.

After this chapter, you will get clarity and be able to identify any limiting beliefs that may be holding you back in your dating life, in flirting, in creating those connections, and in igniting the spark in your date. I will teach you how to take those limiting beliefs and shift them to something lifegiving. You'll become a master at throwing your limiting beliefs to the curb. You'll have complete confidence in knowing who you are created to be in your relationships. Then, we will establish absolute clarity on what you want to accomplish. Without clarity there's confusion. After we set those three things up and you accomplish them, you can move on to the details of flirting. And that's the really fun part!

Let's get started! Grab your journal, grab a cup of tea or glass of wine, and meet me back here.

I encourage you to do these journaling prompts on a regular basis, especially if you are wanting to accomplish a goal. I recommend you continue journaling every day until you hit those goals. This method helps because our mindset is important when it comes to success, and when it comes to success in relationships we are often ingrained with things that happened to us in the past that hinder our success today. I can't stress enough how important it is to set your mind up for success. If I could teach you only one thing, it would be to work on your mindset so that you can be successful in all areas of your life, including relationships and dating. Mindset is where it all begins. I promise you, when you set your mind up for success and do the inner work, you will be amazed at the shift that happens in your daily life. The high value men or women that you're looking for will start showing up in your life. When we do that inner work and that mindset work—that's when miracles happen.

Now, let's conquer those limiting beliefs. If you follow me online, you've probably heard me talk about limiting beliefs. I 110% believe in the power of shifting your mindset into something more powerful. A mindset that's grounded in truth. Limiting beliefs are something that we often don't realize we have complete control of. In reality, we can take total control over all limiting beliefs. We are so used to those limiting beliefs over the years that they're naturally ingrained in us. It could go as far back as our childhood and how we perceive relationships in flirting and dating. We all grew up in different homes, we all grew up with different types of parents who maybe had different types of relationships. Some of us grew up with single moms and didn't know our father. Some of us grew up with a healthy view of marriage, while some of us grew up with an abusive parent or an alcoholic parent. There's so many different family dynamics. You never know what was ingrained early on in our mindset during childhood. By the age of seven, we start to really project those beliefs into our whole lifestyle without even knowing it. Which is why it's so important to identify and recognize anything in our childhood that was a limiting belief, as these are holding us back from having the greatest relationship of our lifetime.

For example, I'll share my story. I had so many limiting beliefs from my childhood that I didn't even realize I was bringing them into my relationships. My parents got divorced when I was about eight years old. My father left my mom for another woman. It was one of the most painful periods of my life, and I still remember that day clearly. From that moment on, my dad never chose me and my brother. He always chose whatever woman was in his life at the time, and that created a lot of pain in my young heart. During high school and college my relationships were toxic, I never knew what a healthy relationship looked like, though I had a picture of a healthy relationship from seeing my grandparents together. They were married for over sixty years and had a beautiful relationship that I admired. My grandfather would always dance around the kitchen with my grandmother. I nicknamed them kissy face ma and pa because they were always kissing. How romantic to be married that long and still be madly in love.

But instead of mirroring my grandparents' behavior, I tended to date men who displayed my father's behavior; extremely charismatic but not reliable or faithful. It was like I was attempting to change them and make them stay with me and love me by trying to heal the experience that happened in my childhood. I had to recognize that after my divorce I was the common denominator in all these relationships. I always dated the bad boy type—handsome, charismatic, outgoing, and fun, but I always ended up heartbroken. It always ended up badly.

Then, something hit me one day; that I was choosing these relationships, I was attracting these relationships. I knew I had to do something different to make a change in my life, and that's when I started doing all the mindset and inner work. I began to heal my past and shift those limiting beliefs into something that was true about me. Now I have the healthiest and most amazing relationship I've ever had.

We have to go back and look at what happened in our childhood. What were the stories that we were told? What did we see? What did we experience? Then we need to take a look at our past relationships. How did we perceive relationships then? What about our perception of flirting? Were the past relationships healthy? Were they abusive? Did they lack love? Do they lack faithfulness? Do they lack flirting and playfulness? What did they lack that did not work? Why are we attracted to that pattern of relationships? What kind of limiting beliefs did we start to form from our past relationships or childhood, maybe even past rejections. Write it all down. Journal it out in detail. This is where it's important to get crystal clear on your limiting beliefs and perceptions regarding relationships. This is the point where you will begin to recognize any dating patterns.

Now, some people form limiting beliefs because they were rejected from past dates or past relationships. For instance, someone might have told you that you're not good enough or you're not pretty enough or maybe they said you're not fun, or whatever it might be; those statements are simply not true. However, often, we let those statements stick in our subconscious, and we continue to believe them. Then we bring them into how we interact with others, how we flirt, and how we interact with new dates. We put up walls around us. We repeat old patterns that no longer serve us and our highest self. Therefore, it is important to recognize anything that was said in our past that we still hang on to regarding relationships, dating, and flirting. Maybe we were told flirting is done a certain way or it's not what a classy woman does. None of those statements are true. Of course, there can be over-the-top, slutty, or creepy flirting. However, there's a way to be classy and attractive about it—the type of flirting that attracts the right type of person and keeps the ones with wrong intentions away. We will dig deeper into that later in the book.

So what were you told? How do you perceive your past relationships or what happened in your past relationships? What do people tell you? What statements do people make about you? What statements do people label you with that made you form limiting beliefs? These are things we were taught about love, relationships, dating, and communication. It's about how we perceive ourselves from past experiences.

Do you have high self-confidence or does it need work? These are limiting beliefs that we can carry when we try to approach people and create new relationships. These are things that keep us stuck in unhealthy dating patterns. How we carry ourselves, the energy that we put into the room, and how we attract other people is shown through what we truly believe about ourselves and our value. Sometimes we are taught all the negative things about love, relationships, and communication. How many times have you heard someone say, "There's no more good men out there," or "men are only looking for a hookup." These are damaging, limiting beliefs. Girl, don't listen to your bestie or a family member who talks bad about the opposite sex. That's just setting you up for failure. Only take advice from people in flourishing relationships.

I want you to just think about that for a second, I want you to start recognizing any limiting beliefs that came up in your life from your past relationships in childhood. We're going to take a moment to journal all this and really dig deeper into it. But the next step in this is to take those limiting beliefs and shift them to truth. Take every limiting belief around flirting, dating, and relationships, and you're going to make that shift. We can't create success in any area of our dating and relationship life if we don't recreate what is true, what is beautiful, what is designed within us. If you don't take anything else from this book but shifting your mindset, then that's a huge success.

Shifting our mindset is so important. We were created by the most high God, I know He created you with a purpose. I know that you are beautiful, and what He created was meant to shine.

When I was growing up, I didn't know that. I didn't know my true worth, I didn't know my true beauty. I didn't know that I was created with a purpose to find a man who would also honor my divine purpose. It's important that we step back and think about, "Okay, how was I created? Why was I created?" Repeat after me, "I was created with a great purpose, I was created absolutely beautiful. I was created to live a life full of love—to be loved." Now those are powerful truths. Thus, we need to remove all of those limiting beliefs around that purpose, and ask for what is ultimately true.

We start by taking each limiting belief and writing a true statement. Start by journaling it, write each limiting belief down and then begin to feel it. Why do you have this limiting belief? Who told you this? Why is it still there? Now, beside each limiting belief write why this isn't true. On one side write the limiting beliefs around flirting, relationships, and dating. Next, find your top three—what beliefs do you think about the most often? It could be someone told you that no man or woman will ever love you, you're not pretty enough, you're not sweet enough, or whatever other statements were made. What are those limiting beliefs that you still struggle with? Write those down. I want you to sit in it for a minute. Often, we need to sit in what we have buried into our subconscious. We need to get it out so that we can feel it, work on it, and get past it. Then we can heal from it and move forward and become something greater because of it.

Next, on the opposite side of the page you're going to take each one of the limiting beliefs and replace it with a life-giving statement. Write down the reasons why those original beliefs are not true and turn it into a statement of truth and affirmation. For example, if your limiting belief is "there are no more good men out there," the statement of truth will be "there are plenty of good men out there, and the right one is being prepared for me now."

After you go through all the limiting beliefs, I want you to think about anything that may have caused rejection in your past. We have all experienced rejection at some point. Now journal it out. It doesn't matter if it's something little, the priority is to get all this relationship yuck out. You might be *thinking this is a lot of work to get started with this book*, but these exercises are designed to help you have more self-confidence as we go through the book and you practice the actionable flirting steps. The more self-confidence you have, the better your dating and flirting experience will be. Throughout this book you will have homework; actionable items to complete, including flirting and making new connections. That's why it's important that you get all the limiting belief yuck out before we start. I want you to get out there with confidence, clarity, and intention throughout your journey of finding 'the one.'

Rejection could have given you low confidence to flirt, but what's the truth? The truth is that person who rejected you was not meant for your journey, and that's okay! I look at rejection as a hidden blessing. I know it's God's way of putting me on my highest self's path and purpose. What's not meant for you is not meant for you, and there's a reason for that. Yes, rejection can cause all kinds of heartbreak, emotions, and insecurities. However, when I think back to the times I've been rejected, I can clearly see how the person who rejected me was not meant for my whole story. They were not meant for my next chapter, and there's a higher reason for that person leaving my life. When I think of each person who is not in my life anymore, I can see clearly why they were removed. They didn't support the highest version of myself and where I am today. You will eventually understand that reason too. It may take time, but rejection is always a hidden blessing in some sense.

Why would we want to give the time of day to someone who rejects us? We are far more worthy than that! Instead, turn that rejection into "What is the hidden blessing behind this rejection?" There's protection in rejection! For example, perhaps that rejection has put you on the path to find that right person, to find your soulmate, the love of your life. Turn that rejection into some type of truth. Go through all those rejections and limiting beliefs and create an empowering, life-giving statement that speaks truth into your life.

What would the highest version of yourself tell you about each statement? I'm sure she wouldn't encourage you to continue to think those limiting thoughts. When I'm working with my clients, we go through these exact prompts to help uplevel their mindset to begin dating successfully. We go much deeper and dig into everything that has held them back from experiencing the best dating life. I recommend focusing on one a day so that you can really step in and tackle it. Whenever one of those limiting beliefs start to creep up, immediately replace it with your life-giving statement. After a while, this will become a habit and those limiting beliefs won't live inside your mind for long. This step is so vital to a successful dating life and future relationships that it cannot be skipped. We all have limiting beliefs, and now is the time to overcome them.

Once you've completed the limiting belief exercise, it's time to move to the next step, which is clarity. After you've gone through the limiting beliefs, you know who you are now, you have your affirmations, you know your absolute truth, your purpose, and you know you are worthy of finding that life partner. Now I want you to get crystal clear about your purpose. What is your ultimate goal for reading this book? What is your ultimate goal in finding a partner? Is it just to flirt and have a good time? Is it to find your lifelong match? It could be any of these reasons. However, I choose to think that most of you are seeking the path to find your soulmate. I think that's the goal of 99.9% of everyone reading this book. Therefore, that's what we need to accomplish.

Now we are going to get super-duper clear. Flirting is, of course, about having fun. But it's also about having that end goal in mind, which is finding and connecting with your soulmate. I want you to become perfectly clear on what you want. Now, you're going to journal about your purpose and it needs to be direct and detailed. It needs to be so detailed that if your soulmate walked through the door, you would be certain they are 'the one.' It's time to ignite your "it factor." You are going to be successful at this, you will be irresistible, people will automatically be drawn to you, you're going to ignite that it-factor within you so that you will catch his attention.

For this journal prompt, the goal is to become crystal clear and get rid of any junk or baggage. Instead, we're living with purpose and dating with intention every single day. If you don't date with purpose it can cause you to repeat unhealthy dating patterns. When we don't have a clear plan with set boundaries we tend to attract the type of people we've always attracted. Like the incredibly handsome bad boys who lead us down the road to the heartbreak hotel. However, when we have more clarity and intention, it's easier for us to stop the relationship at the red flags instead of blindly following his lead. You know you want to find your soulmate who is a high-value partner, who practices integrity and has all the high-quality attributes that you've been missing in men before, right? Those are all of the things that are important to create that long term healthy relationship. The ultimate goal.

So, take out your journal and write down "My Ideal Relationship" at the top of the page. Have you ever found one person who has stayed married for most of their life because of height, hair color, or skin color? Probably not. If so, then you would be the first person to ever tell me that, and I've been a matchmaker for a long time. So, I want you to get rid of that idea that a perfect partner is based on physical traits. He might have gray hair and be 5'10" instead of that tall dark and handsome 6'2" man you saw at the gym. I want you to focus on heart-centered characteristics. Of course, you have to be attracted to him, but the heart-centered characteristics are what will create the lifelong soulmate love. I want you to be clear and detailed about the partner who will create that long-term relationship with you. We're done giving time and energy to all the bad boys and emotionally unavailable men. It's time to attract those high-quality men with long-term relationship virtues.

Begin by listing out five characteristics that are extremely important to you. What are those characteristics that will create a long-term healthy relationship? For example, it could be integrity, faith, family-orientated, or a heart for giving back. Next, journal about what life looks like with this person. What is your everyday life going to look like with your partner? What do your weekends look like? Do you want to travel? Do you want to volunteer together? Do you want to own a lake house? Do you want to grab coffee and have brunch every Sunday morning? What does that look like to you? I want you to close your eyes right now, get super clear, and sit there for a minute and think about what your life is going to look like with him—visualize it. Are you going to have a house in the country or a house in a city with two kids? Just start thinking about how you see life with your partner, then write it down.

I want you to be open about the height, hair color, and even the age range; some people get so focused on the physical qualities that they miss great matches. God doesn't always deliver the perfect plan in a perfectly wrapped gift box. We have to be open about how it's delivered and what it looks like. I've heard people say, "I'm only going to date someone who is five years older than me." But what if your perfect partner is seven years older than you? Are you really going to give up the chance of meeting the love of your life for a few years? I'm not saying you have to go twenty years older, but leave it open a little bit. Journal it out, and write about your future partner. Now that you're perfectly clear on what it looks like to be with your partner, what it feels like to be with your soulmate, and what your future looks like with your life match, you should now have more clarity around dating and relationships. Clarity helps us date with deeper intention and purpose. We tend to spend less energy on men who don't meet our core quality needs when we're crystal clear about what we want and our future.

Congratulations! You have journaled out your purpose in what you want to accomplish with this book! This book is not just about flirting, it's also about getting you to that end goal of finding your life partner. Now you're crystal clear on what you want in a mate, you tackled the limiting beliefs and replaced them with the absolute truth about who you really are, you know who you truly want as a partner, and you have envisioned the life you want to start living. All of this work has led you to the moment of being ready to get out there, date with purpose, while being playful, flirty, and attracting those amazing high-quality dates.

This is where the fun begins!

Chapter Two is going to be all about the science of flirting. It's such a fascinating topic! I can't wait to dig in with you. So grab your journal again and get ready to learn all about what really makes us flirt and how to do it.

THE SCIENCE BEHIND FLIRTING AND IDENTIFYING YOUR FLIRT STYLE

Chapter Two is all about the science of flirting. It's one of my favorite chapters in the book. When I made the course "The Art of Flirting," this module became so long that I had to break it up into two parts. I wasn't expecting to include so much information, but I didn't want to cut anything out either. In the first chapter, we talked about setting the foundation to be successful, getting crystal clear, and healing any limiting beliefs. Setting that foundation is so important to set yourself up for success. So don't skip any steps. You'll need to complete each one to truly see the benefits of the book.

Now, let's get into the science of flirting! Did you know there's a whole science behind why humans flirt, the styles of flirting, and the personalities of flirting? Before I was a matchmaker I had no clue that flirting had a science to it. I just thought it was when people made subtle moves toward another person by touching their arm, leaning into them, and saying flirtatious things. However, it's so much more than that! There's various components that create the science of flirting. I'm going to back each one up in the upcoming chapters. But let's go through some touchpoints of what makes up the science of flirting first. It's such a fascinating subject that I knew I had to share it with everyone! I feel like this is a major component of why people misunderstand human interaction and how to use it to enjoy the dating journey and find their lifelong partner. There's no magic solution to finding your lifelong partner. However, when you learn the key factors in how humans interact and the science behind it, you'll attract higher quality partners quicker and with more ease. You'll no longer waste your time on people who don't exhibit high quality characteristics, and you'll date with more intention and purpose. It saves so much time in the dating world. You become quick to recognize inauthentic behavior or flirting techniques that are not with the best intentions.

This topic is so important because when you're trying to meet new people it can become filled with anxiety or discouragement. My hope with this book is that you gain more confidence and understanding around who you are. That you walk into a room knowing your worth and stop repeating negative dating patterns. It's time to uplevel, babe! And I'm here to walk you through it.

I've talked to thousands of singles, and the majority don't feel comfortable approaching someone in public. They expect the other person to approach them if they're interested, but the reality is the other person is probably thinking the same thing. So no one approaches each other and a connection is lost. It's also easy to get sidetracked by an attractive charmer who comes across your path when you're trying to attract the right high-quality person, which is how we end up in relationships that are emotionally unavailable. We end up repeating negative dating patterns, leaving us wondering why we can't find the one. I want you to set the intention right now that you're only going to attract high-quality dates and be true to yourself. You're not going to attract the same type of people who leave you heartbroken and uncommitted. Make the declaration and journal that exact intention out. Make the declaration that you will only attract high quality commitment minded dates!

So, at this point, you might be wondering, *When are we going to get to the juicy stuff?* Don't worry, I'm going to teach you how to flirt in a classy and fun way by tuning into your personality style! Have you noticed how flirts sometimes get a bad reputation? That should not be the case. The assumption that flirts are slutty or obnoxious is such a myth! As human beings we were created to have fun, to communicate, and when you combine the two; that's all part of flirting. I'll get into that in more detail so that you can take your own personality style and use it to flirt to the best of your ability. I'll also show you how to spot different flirting styles so when you're out you can recognize when someone's flirting with you. It might not be the same flirting style as you, so you might not even notice that they're actually flirting! Which is why we need to study other flirting styles; it can help you to communicate better, be more aware, and be more mindful when you're out meeting new people. You'll have an inside look at how people interact. They most likely won't know the insider matchmaker secrets, but you're going to know them all after reading this book.

And that's why I am beyond excited to teach you! It's like part of my little black book on matchmaking. This subject fascinates me and I just love talking about it and teaching others about it. I believe that if people were more mindful about human behavior and interaction, dating wouldn't be so hard. Instead, the journey would be full of fun, self-exploration, and enjoyment.

I've always loved watching people when I'm out. I love to see how different people flirt and how they interact on dates. When you know all of this, it can set you up for success when it comes to dating. It teaches you how to communicate better, how to interact with people more effectively, and how to have more confidence when you're out looking for that one. Not only that—it also teaches you how to interact with your future partner. Your future partner is going to have their own flirting style, just like they're going to have their own love language. And when you know those things about your partner, you can play off of it and enhance the relationship connection. When we really dig deep and try to understand our partner on a deeper level we create a healthier long-term relationship.

So, are you ready to dig into all the details of flirting?

Flirting is actually like testing the waters to see if the person is worth pursuing. For example, you don't just walk up and say, "I'm attracted to you." That would be a slightly creepy style of approaching someone. Well, some people might actually like that approach if done in the right way. However, most people will likely not just go up to someone and say, "I'm attracted to you!" And then like magic it works and you land the date. How many times has it worked when a guy approaches you at a bar with a cheesy pick-up line? I think it's safe to say not often. Usually, that's not how things work. Attraction is slowly built, and flirting enhances the attraction and magic.

Attraction should be built upon in small doses, and flirting is the best way to do that. If we show a person a large dose of attraction and we're totally over the top about it, we might scare the person away. There has to be some mystery and curiosity behind the attraction phase. It's important to reveal those attraction levels in small doses while creating the new connection. The mystery and curiosity create more chemistry and builds connection. It's an important phase of any relationship and can't be skipped. And you can flirt while doing it, which makes it even more fun.

There's so many different ways to flirt. You can flirt with someone with a gesture as simple as a touch or how you hold your body. A topic we'll cover in Chapter Four is body language, which is a huge indicator of flirting. For example, if your arms are crossed and you look standoffish, that's definitely not flirting. That's like saying 'don't approach me, I'm unapproachable.' However, if your arms are open and you're turned toward that person, that's a way to say 'I'm approachable, talk to me.' It's also a subtle way of flirting and giving the green light for the person to continue the conversation. We'll go over some definite signs of body language and what you can do while out and about with simple things, like how you can hold yourself to be more approachable. Body language plays a huge part in flirting and attraction levels. So much so that if your body language is off, then you're less likely to be approached or even get the date.

Another key way to determine flirting factors is attention. Who are we giving our attention to? Do we lean toward or away from someone? Are we drawn to that person? Do we get closer to that person as the night goes on? These can all be signals that we're flirting. Sometimes we're completely unaware of it.

Another factor of flirting is eye contact. When someone maintains eye contact with you, or you keep catching them gazing at you from across the room, that can be another sure sign they are attracted to you. We're going to go deeper into each one of these, because it's not always obvious how people use specific signs. Mindfulness when you're out and interacting with someone is a crucial step to picking up on flirting and connection cues.

We want to focus on the reasons to flirt and also what we need to do with the person we find attractive. Be mindful of the fact that some people use flirting for the wrong reasons. We've all met the creepy guys who try to flirt just to get someone in bed. I don't want you to get stuck in the patterns of flirting with the wrong people. And I don't want you to get stuck in the patterns of flirting with people who have the wrong intentions. I know most of you reading this book want to find a long-term partner. So, we need to set the intention and focus on finding the people who have the right intentions when it comes to flirting and dating. Everybody has a hidden motivation when they're flirting, make sure it's the right one.

So, what makes up flirting? Did you know that it's partially about social intelligence? There are all kinds of psychological reasons behind it and how we were created as humans. I'm not a scientist, or a psychologist where I can dig in deep into the social intelligence portions of it; however, I'm a matchmaker who has studied human interactions for over a decade and have found what works and what doesn't. It's fascinating how we're made up and how we interact in different cultures, generations, countries, and eras. Ten years ago, flirting was slightly different, because we didn't have the digital technology that we do today. Today, most people begin the flirting process online. Go back ten, twenty, or hundred years ago and flirting was completely different. Go as far back as the 1800s and check out how they flirted. The old-school way of flirting was intentional and on purpose. Throughout generations, people have known how to get the attention of a potential partner. For example, a woman in the 1800s might drop her handkerchief and have the man pick it up. Times have changed drastically, and things are vastly different than just dropping a hanky. Today, people are sliding into dms instead of dropping a handkerchief to get attention. However, the social intelligence behind it is the same, just different in actions across the generations.

The world is full of people who interact differently based on the culture they live in. Our culture can determine how we pick partners and what makes us flirt with certain people versus others. Flirting is made up of fifty percent body language. You're flirting with your body language more than any other thing; any other action or any words that you're saying. So, the first step to becoming mindful is paying attention to what your body language is saying. For successful flirting techniques, an emphasis would be made on body language. Thirty-eight percent of flirting is made up of your tone and the speed of your voice. That is very interesting to me because it's proven that it's less about what we say—only seven percent of what we say actually makes up flirting. We could say the stupidest things and there is less focus on that than if we say it with a good tone and speed of speaking. The main factors of flirting then are your body language combined with the tone and speed of your voice. So just keep that in mind. When you're out and about and you think, *I don't know what to say to him, I don't know how to approach him*, go back to this because it doesn't really matter. It's only seven percent of what we say that actually makes up the flirty part of that interaction. So, just ensure you have open body language with a positive tone and even speed of your voice. And focus less on what you have to say or what you're going to say. That should put some interacting fears to rest!

The most significant characteristic of flirting is your body language and your speaking style. However, studies have also shown that you also have to have a well-groomed appearance. So, when you combine those three things, your flirting style goes off the charts. A lot of people think flirting is natural to people. They believe that it's what you say, your laugh, or it's the cheesy flirty things that you see in movies. In reality, it's your body language, speaking style, and a well-groomed appearance. A lot of people miss these key components when they try to flirt or approach someone. They get scared and feel timid, but really they can relax and do it with ease.

The first step is to focus on your body language. What energy are you putting out into the room? When you walk in a room, people will either be drawn to you or not. It's not about if you're the most attractive person there, it's how you captivate and grab the attention with the energy you radiate. Energy is everything. And when our energy is on point, our body language radiates with it. Our eyes light up, our skin is glowing, and we walk with confidence.

I do want to point out just some simple things about your body language, just so you have these little tips in the back of your mind.

When it comes to body language and flirting, the most important thing for you to know is that body language is how you present yourself. So, if you're closed off with your arms crossed and you have resting bitch face, you're not putting out the vibes of flirting. Instead you are giving off the vibes of, "Don't talk to me, don't approach me, I don't want to talk to anybody." It is therefore so important when you are out and about with your friends, or you're even by yourself, to be mindful of the vibe you're putting out into a room. If you want to meet the one, then you have to be mindful about what you're attracting when you walk into a room. You might not necessarily be looking for a partner at that moment, but you never know when you're going to find that person. So it's important to be mindful about how you're presenting yourself wherever you are so that you look approachable and attract the right type of people.

Some simple tips to get started:

- Learn not to cross your arms in any fashion and keep them open.
- Keep your arms and posture straight.
- Don't keep your hands folded, keep your hands open and your shoulders up.
- When you're talking to someone you may be interested in, it's important to have your shoulders facing them, this shows that you're interested.

I can always tell when people are on dates if they're interested in who they're with or not. I can also tell if the dates are going smoothly and if they're going to go on a date with that person again. I simply observe their body language and their conversation style. If you're even slightly interested in your date you want to make sure that you're showing positive body language. Because if you don't you might not get that next date. Always remember, arms open, hands up, don't keep your hands or arms crossed. Keep your shoulders facing them, your feet pointing toward them. If you're on a date and someone's feet and shoulders are not facing you, there's a disconnect there. Maybe they're not interested or they feel insecure. However, the good news is if you're interested in them you can possibly change their interest level in you. Some people are just closed off when they first meet someone. Remember, body language is vital in interaction.

Step two is your tone of voice. You need to keep a moderate tone and a consistent pace of speech. For me, I usually talk fast, especially when I'm excited about something or I'm having fun. So, instead, you just take a breather and remember to get back to the consistent tone and pace of speech in order to ensure that you're not too loud, you're not too soft, but you're consistent. Pay attention to your tone. Does the tone of your voice sound standoffish? Does it sound like you may have a bad attitude or you're snobby? Be aware of that, because that person is paying attention to your tone and how you're talking to them. Some people sound annoyed when they're talking. Has anybody ever said, "Your tone of voice sounds like you're mad or you're upset"? Really pay attention to that because it could be affecting your dates.

Step three, practice active focus listening. Another aspect of connection and flirting that people are usually unaware of is that active focus listening is actually a type of flirting style. It's very powerful! Plus, there's nothing you have to really do to flirt but just listen to what that person has to say. How easy is that to up your attraction level? While you're making eye contact, you're also listening to them. I mean you're really listening to what they have to say, you're not just letting them ramble, you're listening, you're asking questions, you're engaging. They can feel how interested you are in what they have to say. That speaks far more volume than someone walking in who's drop-dead gorgeous. When a person can actively listen and be interested in what someone has to say, that is more attractive than the most gorgeous person in the room. You just became the person they want to continue to talk to throughout the night.

If you're like me and have trouble focusing, or if you have ADHD, you might need to practice tuning in and focusing on conversations. Start practicing with your family and friends. It won't only help you in dating situations but it will improve your other relationships too. It's a sexy quality when someone listens with interest and engages with you in an authentic conversation. Intelligence and listening is so much more attractive than someone who doesn't care what you say.

What about all the myths around flirting? For example, the saying "When you play hard to get, you get the guy." That may be true, but what you're really doing is setting up the stage to play games. I'm not a fan of all the books and advice out there that preach things like, "Why bitches get the man and the ring" or dating rules like "Wait three days to call him." I just can't stand inauthentic dating advice. It sets you up for relationship failure. That's just setting the entire relationship up to play games like it's normal. When you play games to get the guy, you attract what you put out there... a guy who plays games. That's an immature and unhealthy way of getting a man, especially if you want to find a relationship that is long-term, lifelong, and healthy. Why are you playing games to get into a relationship? That's setting it up for failure from day one. So, the myth to the method of flirting that when you play hard to get you get the guy is simply not true. Now, I'm not implying that you should jump into a relationship. What I mean is don't play the games of "Okay, I'm not going to call them for two days," or "I'm not going to text them for four hours." I'm not advising you to give yourself away in the physical sense, what I mean is you can start making that emotional connection and allowing it to flow naturally without throwing up roadblocks. Communication and connection are key when it comes to relationships. Don't play a game so hard that they give up or that they can't even communicate with you in a healthy, normal, and consistent manner. Studies show that game playing is a complete myth when it comes to creating long-term healthy relationships. So stop playing hard to get if you want the authentic, healthy, high-quality man.

Myth number two is there's only one way to flirt. When I was growing up, I always thought flirting was kind of the same: you giggle, you touch his arm, you say little flirty things, and you laugh at his jokes. The truth is people flirt differently. There are different flirting personality styles. A lot of times someone may be flirting and we'll be clueless because we don't see it as flirting. They're just using their natural flirting style. People just do not flirt the same. Don't get upset if you think your boyfriend or girlfriend isn't flirting with you or being playful. He or she might be but in their own way. Just like they have their own love language, they also have their own flirting language.

If you haven't read the book *The Five Love Languages* I highly recommend that you get it because it shows another important aspect of relationships. I believe that when you understand how people respond and interact, it can change your relationships. It will change the dynamic of dating and creating long-term relationships for you because you will begin to understand the deeper levels of how humans interact in intimate relationships. Understanding someone's love language will give you a glimpse into their soul and how they respond to love. For example, they might love to give gifts or give words of affirmation but may not do many acts of service. Acts of service is just not their love language, but they show love by giving you words of affirmation. Love languages can absolutely tie into their flirting style. Some flirts love to give compliments or say sweet words, but someone else might not flirt that way. You might not think they are flirting back with you because you're just speaking two totally different flirt languages.

The bottom line is—everyone responds differently to flirting. Not one person is made up the same with the same personality, the same perceptions, or the same flirting styles. When we start to understand and accept this about others, we start to relate and connect better to those around us. Everyone has different personalities and communication styles, so how we perceive things will be different. We have to remember that some people might not respond the same to flirting as you would expect them to, and that's totally okay! Don't get disappointed, it's just that they're a different person with different styles of communicating, flirting, and perceiving people around them. Don't feel rejected, they might actually like you. Or they're just not your person. If there's no investment from them into getting to know you in return, don't continue to pursue the interaction. It's as simple as that. Save your energy for someone who will reciprocate the interaction and invest in getting to know you too.

Now, let's talk about flirting styles and the five different styles of flirting. Every person has a different flirting style. In this book you'll be able to identify your unique style. If you're thinking, *I'm not going to identify my style because I don't even know how to flirt!* Well, the good news is you're already flirting but you're just not aware of it. Even if you're shy and introverted you still have your own unique flirting style. And this is the part where we learn all the different styles that people might have. It is important to learn how to recognize the different styles because when you're out and about you want to be able to know if someone is flirting with you and if they're interested. You also want to understand your own flirting style and how you can improve it to create stronger connections. I'll also throw some tips on how you can create other flirting styles so that you can make sure that cutie catches the vibe you're putting out.

The first flirting style is physical. These are the people who smile often, are less verbal, but they give more compliments. They like to touch, they use positive body language, it's all about their physical appearance and how they present themselves. This is more like the person who comes over and touches your hand or moves your hair out of your face. They're the ones always smiling and look approachable and friendly. Their body language is very positive. Their arms are open and not crossed, they are turned in toward you, and they're giving you attention. The physical flirting style is usually pretty obvious. It's easier to recognize because it's the stereotypical way we perceive flirting. Could this be your flirting style? Do you tend to smile a lot? Do you gradually lean in for a light touch? Is your body language positive, open, and you like to give compliments? If you answered yes to those questions, then your flirting style most likely is physical. Are you also a words of affirmation person? If so, this correlates with the physical flirting style. You love to get and give compliments. As we go through each of these, identify if your personality or love language matches your flirting style.

The second flirting style is traditional. The people who use this flirting style see it more as a game to gain the attention of someone they're attracted to. They see it as a way to catch the girl or guy, and it's a fun feat for them. Women who use the traditional flirting style usually won't make the first move. They often expect the man to make the first move. Another thing that they like to do is to lean into someone. It's a more traditional or classic way of flirting, similar to that of how they flirted decades ago. They might lean into the person as they're talking to them or maybe employ a little verbal teasing. Remember in elementary school the verbal teases from some of the boys? You may have thought that boy was being annoying, but really it was likely he actually liked you. Why do people correlate light teasing with flirting? Teasing someone you like is done with affection and lightheartedness. It usually brings a smile to someone's face, some laughter, and you feel at ease being around them.

The third flirting style is sincere. Yes there's a "sincere" flirting style! These people are actually flirting, but they're sincere at doing it and flirting in a more unsuspecting way. They're great listeners and they're extremely focused on getting to know someone. They're genuinely in tune with what the other person is saying and sincere about what they're saying in response. They show interest by asking questions about who they are, what they like to do, they're passions, and what lifestyle they choose to live. They're focused on that person and sincere in getting to know them. They don't do the whole smiley, touchy, feely type thing or lots of verbal compliments. They don't see it as a game but instead a genuine authentic conversation. They might not show interest in body language but instead in their focus on you. And the best part is that they're completely authentic about it. So if you're talking to someone and they act like this, they might actually be flirting with you unbeknownst to you. You might just think they're being nice and a great conversationalist, but in reality this could be their flirting style. Therefore, it's important to be mindful about each flirting style, as you will start to pick up on them as you date. It will be easier to identify if your partner is flirting rather than assuming they're not being playful or flirty, and you get a deeper understanding of others as you recognize each person's flirting style.

The fourth flirting style is politeness. People with polite flirting styles are more formal, polite, and classy. However, they can seem distant because they like to play it cool. Sometimes it appears as if they're cold or emotionally uninvolved, but that's just how they are, that's how they flirt. They might even like to lean back instead of leaning into you during a conversation. You won't see any of the physical or traditional flirting with a polite flirting style. They usually remain sophisticated and classy, like it's no big deal. Think of the polite flirting style as relaxed and mysterious. They don't like to give away that they're actually into you.

The fifth flirting style is playful. The playful flirting styles are the natural flirts who love to have fun and be playful. They might pinch you, joke around with you, and they love to laugh. The playful style can be more obvious too. They are more outgoing and engaging and just love having fun. I'm sure you could spot one of these flirts immediately.

Don't forget to be mindful of all the flirting styles we talked about: physical, traditional, sincere, polite and playful. Now you can easily identify different flirting styles when you're out. You can also combine some of these flirting styles to show your flirting side off.

Someone who has a sincere flirting style is more likely to think someone is flirting with them who mirrors their flirting style. However, you could throw a few of the different styles in together to really connect with someone! You've got to make sure that the person you're attracted to knows you're flirting with them. Don't be over the top and try every flirting style in one move. Take it easy and make it fun. For example, you can smile, touch them on the arm, and listen intently to what they have to say. Pick a few out so that you can create deeper connections with the person who catches your eye.

You might be wondering, *But, Amanda, what do men really prefer?* I know sometimes we think that men prefer the most attractive person in the room, but that isn't true at all! It's not about being the most attractive person in the room, it's about being the most approachable. Women who smile and make eye contact are more likely to be approached than the most attractive woman in the room. That is what men actually prefer when it comes to flirting.

When it comes to attraction levels, the person who is available, approachable, makes eye contact, smiles, and looks friendly is the one men mostly prefer. They will more than likely approach the friendly sociable woman over the most attractive woman. When you're out and about, be mindful of how you're coming across to others. Make sure you're having a good time, smile, and have open body language, this makes you instantly more approachable.

Men also prefer more direct approaches, they don't like games. They like to be approached directly. And how can you do that? We will go over this more, and I'll give you some key examples and actionable tips. Let's say, you're at a restaurant, coffee shop, or bar, and you see someone you'd like to talk to or start a conversation with. You can go up and say, "Hi," start some small talk, but I suggest to not say "Hi" right away, stand by him for a second. You can start a small conversation, and that is a direct approach. You don't have to stand across the room and try to make eye contact awkwardly. Just do the direct approach. Men prefer women ask open ended questions. They feel more bonded when you ask more intimate questions.

So, what are the most attractive flirting features? Well, happiness is the most attractive female expression. This is proven across the board—the most attractive female expression is happiness. It's not who looks the best in the room or who looks like they're hard to get.

However, pride is the most attractive feature for males, and studies show that it is believed that a man with pride looks like he has his stuff together. He is well kept, he is not arrogant and prideful, but he is confident, knows what he wants, and doesn't play games. Imagine that classy, well put together man—this is the most attractive feature for males.

What is the vibe of flirting? Well, the vibe of flirting is definitely fun, spontaneous, confident, and positive. That's the vibe we want to stay in. So, as you go through this book, I want you to remember to stay in this vibe of flirting, which is keeping it fun, keeping it spontaneous. Don't overthink it, stay confident and stay positive. I think positivity is one of the most important qualities to have when you go out and flirt. You need to stay positive, because if you put off a negative energy it instantly sends people away. You don't look approachable and you instantly lose attraction levels. It's therefore important to stay positive when you're out and about and to keep that vibe of flirting. Flirting is all about being positive. It's all about being confident, having fun, and being approachable.

So, when you're out and about, think, *I'm going to meet amazing people*, talk yourself up, give yourself that pep talk, and get out there and stay in that vibe of flirting. I like to ask, "What would the highest version of yourself do? The highest version of yourself who is wanting to meet the man of her dreams? Would you be negative? Would you shut down and be closed off? Would you be having fun? Would you be confident? Would you be positive? Write that question down in your journal. "What would the highest version of myself do in this situation?" I guarantee it would probably be to have fun, to be positive, to be confident. Make sure you always stay in that mindset of whatever your highest version of yourself would be doing. I ask myself that question in every situation, not just in relationships but in my business and with my children with the decisions I make every day, what is the highest version? What would the highest version of myself do? Keep that in your mind as you go out and you're flirting, looking for Mr. or Mrs. Right. Flirting is basically like a checklist to meet new exciting people and have fun. There's nothing that we should put on flirting that is bad or scary. And I know often it is scary, because we don't even know where to start. But we have to remember that practice makes perfect.

You can take different aspects from the different learning styles and apply them to when you're out. If you see someone, go over those flirting styles one more time, remember—physical, traditional, sincere, polite, and playful. Let's say, for instance, you're out and you see someone you are attracted to. Let's take an aspect from the physical flirting style, such as smiling. Make a mental note—you're going to smile often and have fun. Maybe your flirting style is traditional and you think men should always make the first move. I want you to erase that thought, because it's okay for women to make the first move and be classy about it. Erase that thought that men should always make the first move, because that's not always the case, and it doesn't always work that way. Moreover, why would you want to miss out on someone amazing because you want to stick with that traditional flirting style or comfort zone? Now, let's take something from the traditional flirting style; you could lean into that person, move in closer. If your flirting style is sincere flirting, you're a great listener. So, use that to your advantage, you can listen intently and show interest. If you're flirting with politeness, you can take something from that and just be classy, be polite, be nice. If flirting sounds playful, then you're a natural flirt, and you're probably having fun anyway. So, you can take something from that too, if that's not your flirting style, you could be a little playful, a little teasing. Find a way to naturally take something from each flirting style and apply it the next time you're out. You don't have to make it this hard, just do little things each time, because practice makes perfect. Remember, it's just a checklist to meet new exciting people and have fun, because you never know who you're going to meet!

You are going to have some homework, but it's going to be fun and I want you to get it done. This week, do something; go out, go somewhere new, go to a new event, new coffee shop, or a new restaurant and apply this homework. Remember, practice makes perfect.

I know that sometimes it's so hard to get out of your comfort zone. But what is on the other side of your fear? I want you to think about that for a second. What is on the other side of your fear of doing this? Is it finding that perfect person? Is it potentially opening up communication to a great conversation with an amazing person you otherwise would have never met unless you went to the other side of that comfort zone, the other side of that fear? Sometimes, the best things in life are on the other side of fear. So, it's important, for you may discover your potential soulmate, the love of your life. Let's make a pact to get out there and start meeting new people. Because the more people you meet, the closer you are getting to that perfect person. Remember that and maybe make it like a checklist too. You may meet a hundred people who are not right, but after you meet those hundred people, you know that your soulmate is even closer, because you've already gone through all those other people. You know that you're just weeding them out, one by one. Look at it in a more positive aspect; that you are on a mission, and practice makes perfect.

Here's what you're going to do for your homework, you are going out this week, and you're going to put these into action. You're going to practice open body language, no crossed arms, a smile on your face, you're going to turn toward someone when you're talking to them. You don't have to be all up in their face, but just turn toward them. Maybe a flirty touch, like a touch on the arm, a gentle touch on the hand. I want you to listen with focus, ask questions, engage, and really show interest. You never know where it will lead. Make sure that you are paying attention to them and that you're giving them eye contact. Ensure your eyes aren't wandering off to other people in the room but you're actually giving attention to that person. And then, have fun, laugh, and enjoy yourself. Don't ask too serious of questions, you want to keep it light and fun and laugh together. And don't forget proximity, which kind of goes with attention. If you see someone you're attracted to, make your way over to that person or in their area. Don't stay way across the room, but get close enough where you could start to possibly create that conversation.

CHAPTER THREE

CONFIDENCE IS KEY

I am so excited that you've made it to Chapter Two, this chapter is all about confidence. Confidence is key in any social situation. You have to have the confidence to walk into a room and know who you are. It's walking into a room with the confidence that you can and will create connections that are for your highest good. And you'll have the confidence to walk away from any connections that don't serve you without fear of rejection or disappointment. Remember, rejection is protection. So, anyone who doesn't connect with you when you walk in a room or on a date is meant for your protection. You don't want to waste energy on just anybody. Your energy is valuable, sacred, and reserved for those who are meant to serve your highest purpose in life, dating, and relationships. Confidence is key in putting the best version of yourself out there when dating. It's being your authentic self and owning it. Confidence is so key when it comes to dating, that taking this aspect out can lead you into bad dating patterns, unhealthy relationships, and/or not finding a high-level partner. It's important to start putting it into action when you are dating and flirting. Because, again, flirting isn't just about your traditional, flirty laughs and all those flirty behaviors. It's more about confidence, it's about dating as the best version of yourself.

There's a difference between arrogance and confidence. Don't mistake a healthy confidence with arrogance. I don't want you walking in a room and being arrogant. Some people have this arrogant confidence, like they're too good for anyone in the room and they're completely unapproachable. They're not what you would classify as friendly or flirty. They're not the ones who are approached, and that is certainly not what I'm teaching. I'm teaching healthy confidence, where you're approachable, where people want to talk to you, where your energy is so contagious, people just want to be around you. There's a huge difference, please do not confuse the two.

What is healthy confidence when it comes to dating and interpersonal communication? If you've experienced past heartbreak or any relational insecurity it can be hard to regain confidence. I know I've been there. I had the dysfunctional childhood plus the bad relationships that shattered my confidence for many years. I did a lot of healing work to get to the other side of being confident in my authentic self and setting boundaries to keep my mental space safe.

So, let's say you've been through a lot, you don't have that healthy self-confidence, and you have limiting beliefs holding you back. Those limiting beliefs and lies that are telling you you're not worthy enough, you're not pretty enough, you don't have the best personality, or whatever beliefs are holding you back from being the highest version of yourself. We all have many limiting beliefs that we have to conquer, and we have to replace them with healthy beliefs.

Confidence is a mindset, a knowing of who you are. It's not about money, if you wear the best clothes, or if you're the prettiest person in the room. It's all about mindset. That's where confidence comes from; deep within you. And it's important to know that you are worthy of having that healthy confidence. We're all created with a purpose. We're all worthy. The knowledge that we were created with purpose, are worthy of the best relationships, of finding the best love, and of being treated with respect is where our confidence comes from. When we know deep down in our hearts that we are worthy of those things, then our confidence increases. And that's what will change your entire perspective when it comes to approaching people and who you let in your space.

So, if you have any limiting beliefs, let's say from your childhood, from a past relationship, or from someone who put a statement on you that's not true, I want you to immediately tackle that, stop what you're doing and journal it out. Write those limiting beliefs down and why you think you're not worthy enough to have the ultimate healthiest confidence? Then replace those statements with something of truth. On one side put your limiting beliefs and list them. Take some time and really dig into each limiting belief. Go back to childhood, go back to your past relationships. What did the people say about you that created a lower self-esteem? Was it a teacher in elementary school or a bully? I was picked on, first through third grade, because I was so quiet, and those things stuck with me. I still remember the things that those kids said to me. I still remember the toxic statements from past relationships. The thing is; they don't define me, they don't define my story, and they don't define my future. And any toxic statements that someone spoke over you don't define YOU! So, what is it that people said or the limiting beliefs that you have put on yourself to cause your confidence to lower? Write those out on one page and then on another page I want you to write at the top, "Why isn't this true?"

So, if a limiting belief is "You're not good enough for a great relationship" or "you're never good enough," write in detail why that statement is not true.

If you take and tackle each one of those, you'll find that they are just limiting beliefs that someone else put on you or you have created for yourself because of past experiences. So, get out a journal, conquer each limiting belief, and make the decision right now that you'll never believe them again. Continue to go back to your truth statements every day until they are so ingrained in your mind that you don't believe anything else.

Confidence is having that mindset, knowing your true worth, and also being authentic. If you go out today, you might notice that there's a lot of people who don't act authentically, they're putting on a show, they're buying things or doing things to make them feel more worthy. I like nice stuff, too, I'm not saying you can't buy nice things. I'm just saying there's some people who try to overcompensate with buying things or being materialistic. I think something that's really powerful when you're dating and you can be open and authentic with the person across from you. When you can admit your flaws and what you've done wrong. I think that's really powerful, and that way you have a more powerful connection with people. Or I should say, you will have a more powerful connection with authentic people when you are authentic yourself. That's a part of being confident too. You can go into a room and talk to people and be real, you know who you are and no one can change that. You're authentic but can also admit your flaws and be relatable to those around you. You become the ultimate attraction factor.

For instance, I'm divorced and remarried. My divorce is not something that I'm proud of. However, I used that mess to turn it into my message. I can admit that in my twenties I was the poster child for bad relationships. I went through bad relationship after bad relationship. Finally, it hit me, "I'm not just being treated wrong. I'm the common denominator here. I'm attracting these people for a reason. I'm the one who ends up in bad relationship after bad relationship." I can admit that now and say, "Hey, I messed up, I wasn't picking the right people." When I share that with other people, I hope they can relate to me better, and instead of thinking, *She's a matchmaker and has it all together*, they'll think, *Hey, she's human. She's been there too.* When people can relate to you better and feel free to be themselves, it creates a deeper connection. Confidence is about owning who you are despite your faults, and showing up as your authentic self. Because the right people and the higher quality people will relate better and be attracted to people who show up as their authentic self. Someone who owns the mess, shows confidence, and is a hundred percent authentic with who they are. No bs attached.

As you can see, confidence isn't just about your mindset, it's also about being authentic. You are created with divine purpose. Your past mistakes and flaws can be transformed into your superpowers and part of your true beauty. Highlight who you are, own it, and don't put on a show. The person who is attracted to a false perception of you will not love the true you.

Represent your true beauty and let your authenticity come alive, that's when your confidence will shine. You don't have to be someone you're not, that never ends well. Confidence is also knowing who you are and what you deserve. I think a lot of times people who date sometimes settle because they think, "Well, I'm not going to find anybody, I'm going to have to settle for less than what I deserve just to find someone who loves me." That's a limiting belief! You will find your true partner when you start living as the highest version of yourself with authenticity.

When you walk into a room, including on a date, know who you are and what you want. Set those boundaries and intentions of how the highest version of yourself would act. It's not about being the mean girl or being a bitch. It's about having the confidence to know who you are and what you want. I know that whoever I surround myself with is going to be a high-quality person and someone who shares similar values as me, and that is an absolute non-negotiable. So, if the person sitting across from you doesn't have the non-negotiable qualities but they're hot and you continue to date them, you're lacking self-confidence. You see what I'm saying. If that person lacks what you truly want in someone and you still continue to date them because you feel like you need to settle, that's lacking self-confidence. You need to know who you are and what you want.

I want you to stop right here for a moment. I want you to get out your journal and write what you want in a relationship. What are the top five qualities you desire in a partner? What are the values you want in a high-quality partner? These are your non-negotiables. You know what you want and you won't settle for less. When you know this with every bit of your soul, you'll start to own the room when you walk in.

You know you want someone who is loyal, you want someone who has a good sense of humor, you know you want someone who shares the same faith as you; whatever it is—know what you want and don't settle.

I'm not saying you should set your guidelines physically, such as you want a six foot tall man, because God might put someone in your space who is 5'10 or 5'11 and bald. Never be so particular about how someone looks or the physical features of someone that you miss out on the person who is a match for you. I know you have to be attracted to him, but just be open about that.

You know what you want and that you are worthy of it; you are worthy of having that healthy relationship. And once you can let that soak in and really get it, then your confidence will increase. So, get out the journal, write all that you want down, and be clear about it.

I know when you walk into a room, or you walk into a date, it can be nerve-wracking. It can cause anxiety, you get the jitters, and you're sweating, maybe stumbling your words. I still do those things some-times when I'm going into social settings. But I've learned a trick. When you're going into a social setting, and this can be any social setting, let's say you're going out with your girlfriends and you're going to scout the room, see what you can find, or maybe you're going on that first date or second date, whatever it may be, there are some things to increase your confidence you have to do before-hand. You need to create a state of calm before you go out and go on those dates. This will help you to be less anxious and more confident. You have to create that state of calm to create higher confidence when you get there and when he arrives. Here are some things that I like to do. I like to meditate, pray, to sit there in silence and just really create that state of calm. I love to do yoga because it balances and grounds me, and I feel like I can approach an event or someone with more ease. I feel like my brain is at ease, my thoughts have calmed down. Something else I love to do is go for a walk. I love to hike in nature. When I'm in nature by the water I can instantly calm my nerves, calm the anxiety, and it's proven scientifically that hiking, yoga, meditation, and prayer will do all those things.

Also, I want you to be confident before you walk into a date or social setting. Invest in some go-to-outfits, a classy but professional looking outfit, something that you feel great in when you walk into a room, something that inspires you to think, "I felt amazing about myself. This outfit makes me feel amazing." It doesn't have to cost a lot, purchase it from a resell app or a consignment store, or the clearance racks. Invest in some go-to outfits to make you feel great about yourself, because you want to walk in with confidence like you own the place.

Here are some steps to a confident date. When I say you want to create this mindset of confidence, I want you to take this into every social setting and every date you go on, because when someone's confident, you put on a more positive and approachable vibe if all goes together. You have to create the confidence to flirt successfully.

Step one: to feel and look confident on your date is to look your best, get those go-to date night outfits. Be neatly groomed, make sure your nails are done, you have updated hair, a fresh makeup look but do not overdo the makeup. I have been doing this for eight years. I have talked to thousands of men, and no one has said, "I love when she overdoes her makeup and it looks caked on." Not one. Usually they say, "I don't want to date the girl that has way too much makeup on because I feel like she's hiding something, lacks confidence or has a lot of fake stuff going on." Men like the natural look. Now if you like to glam, do wear it, but just make sure it's not overly done, make sure it's updated, it's fresh, it looks good with your features, and it's not caked on, you can do a totally natural, glam look. Be sure you look your best when you walk in, that will increase your confidence instantly.

Step two: Confidence isn't just on the inside, it shows on the outside too. This is when body language comes in. I know we're talking a lot about body language in this book, but it's so key, we have another chapter focused on it. Body language speaks volumes, it talks louder than words sometimes. So you need to make sure that you have a good posture. Practice sitting up straight when you're at your office or when you're at home so it becomes natural and eventually becomes a habit. Have an authentic, fun, friendly, open smile. Make eye contact, as this increases confidence. If you look away because you're nervous, which I used to do all the time, you can practice by making eye contact with yourself in the mirror and proclaim your affirmations out loud. It looks silly at first, but I promise you it works. Make sure you have charm, you're enthusiastic, and you have good body language, because all of that will show that you have confidence, and it will build your confidence as you practice it. A lot of times it doesn't come naturally, so it's these things that we have to continue to practice.

Step three: Create that flirty energy. If you take step one and step two, you start to create flirty energy. Create playfulness and have lighthearted conversations when you're on a date. Never, ever make the conversation too serious, especially on the first and second date. You don't want to scare people off and I see this so often, where people scare their dates off because they want to get straight to the point to see if they agree on serious life issues. Then they don't get the second date. Stay away from all marriage, future children, political, and religious topics. Unless you already know each other's religious and political beliefs I would keep those topics off the table. All those topics should wait until you create that light hearted, at ease environment and have established a bond. I always suggest to always just keep it fun. You're talking about what you like to do on the weekends, your hobbies, amazing travel adventures. Talk about what you like to do around the city.. All those things. But don't bring in the marriage questions and the serious things like "Do you want to get married?" "Do you want to have kids?" "What do you think of the political things going on in the world?" That just gets too serious and too heated sometimes. It's better to keep it light and playful instead. Keep smiling, Make eye contact, ensure your body turns toward the date. Create that flirty energy and give undivided attention, while sparking curiosity. Be curious about your date, ask questions about them. To spark curiosity on your part—don't give them your whole life story since you were a child. Keep them curious so they keep coming back wanting to learn more. There's no reason to give somebody a whole life story on a first date.

Step four: Again, simple is best when it comes to appearance. Working with men and women, I always like to ask them things like "What are they looking for in someone?. The most common response I get is that they prefer someone classy and well put together. So wear something simple and solid that really accentuates your features. Don't wear things that have stripes, patterns or floral patterns. Wear a cute dress or nice top with jeans. Or wear red! It grabs attention, and is known to create that flirty look. Red and pink are good colors for that, but keep it simple. A cute red top with some jeans, some heels, and some light makeup would look really good for a first date!

Put all those steps together, and that creates an atmosphere set up for success. The date setting of flirty, fun, playful and confident. Because you're looking good, and you've created that atmosphere to keep it light hearted and fun!

Okay, so this is a topic I love to talk about. Rejection is protection. Let that soak in for a second. Here's the thing, rejection is going to happen, we have all been hurt by it, we have all experienced rejection in some shape or form in our life. It could be we didn't get the job, didn't get the date, someone broke up with us, a parent or a teacher rejected us, or whatever it may be. If we start to look at rejection with a new mindset and a new perception of what it actually is, everything starts to change, you will start to care less about being rejected and instead look at it like a hidden blessing. Yes, rejection can sting, it definitely does. Because the thing is, we think it's all about us. And really, that's not exactly the case. You know, rejection just means that person who rejected us no longer has a place in our story, and that's okay. It's meant for our highest good, because oftentimes when someone rejects us, we ask, "What's wrong with me? What did I do wrong? Am I not pretty enough? Am I not good enough? Am I not fun enough?" We asked all these questions instead of asking "Why are they not part of my story anymore?" There's usually a good reason for that, I think about past relationships, such as a high school boyfriend who broke up with me for someone else, and I look back now and think, *Oh, thank goodness he did and I did not end up with him! Because my life would not be as good as it is now. I wouldn't have the man and the kids that I have now.* That was definitely a rejection that was protection, the blessing in disguise, that person is no longer a part of my story for a reason. Because my story has a higher better version.

And it is the same for you. If you look back at some past relationships, think about what it would be like to be married to that person and have kids with that person. That can be a scary realization. Remember, that person is just not a part of your story anymore. So, have confidence when you think about it. Rejection can cause us to lose confidence. But we need to make that shift in our mindset that "this rejection happened because they're not a part of my story anymore. I am made to create the highest version of myself, which is yet to come, and they don't have anything to do with that part of my story." Be excited, because what will happen next for you? You will meet that one, that amazing man! Remember, rejection is just protecting you from someone who should not be in your life anymore. You may think, "What's wrong with me?" A lot of times rejection isn't even based on what's wrong with you. It could be a number of things, such as, "This person is not the best partner for me and I need to trust God to protect me from something I don't see."

We need to trust in something that we don't see. The person can just be emotionally unavailable, already in a relationship, too busy for a relationship, not be ready for a relationship, and you don't want to be with someone like that. Just remember that rejection is protection. Write that down, paste it all over your house if you have to. Don't get too caught up in someone not calling you back or ghosting you because they can't communicate. If they're showing that to you now, thank goodness that they are gone. That shows a lack of communication skills. They're lack of communication skills shows you a glimpse into what you're future would look like with them.

Confident women don't need validation, they already know their true worth and beauty. When you're confident, you don't need that validation, you don't care about potential rejection, you already know how worthy you are, you know your true worth, you know your true beauty. You're thankful for any rejection because you know with your whole heart that it was divine protection watching over you. You know with everything within you that it is opening the way for something even better to come your way. If you go out, you will see a lot of men and women not talking to each other, especially if you go to a singles mingle, you'll see a lot of men and women break off into groups. And it's usually the women who go stand somewhere and then the men group up somewhere, but they don't interact. Go out and start looking, because you'll see a lot of men and women not interacting. You'll see people waiting for the other person to make the first move. So, if you want to stand out, you have to have the confidence to start the conversation, because you're already ahead of the game, you are already using this book. You already know some secrets behind how humans interact when they're single. You are also going to be ahead of the game, because you're going to start the conversation, you're going to start the connection and the interaction, you can do it! You have created that confidence level that a lot of people don't have. Confident women don't need validation, they can go start a conversation. And if that man is a complete loser or he's not into you, you don't care, you move on, because you already know your true worth and beauty. You are already in the room, you're shiny, you can start the conversation.

The thing is, most men and women are not your competition, because they are not doing the work. You are doing the work, so you are already ahead of the game. You're out there and you're being completely authentic. Let's say you feel nervous, because it is nerve wracking! It takes practice to get out there and be confident and to approach people. If you feel nervous, call yourself out and laugh about it, because it's most likely that your date or the person you're talking to is just as nervous as you are. And when you're open, it takes the pressure off of you and just makes that conversation a relief and you can talk, laugh, and have a good time without putting on a whole show. When you can call yourself out, people relate to that. They want to connect to you, which in turn makes it a more relaxed atmosphere and a better date

I want you to think about what makes you feel confident? What makes you feel powerful? What makes you feel secure? What makes you feel sexy, open, and loving? I want you to write all that down. What makes you feel that way? After that, I want you to write down what makes you feel afraid? What makes you feel closed off or distressed? And write that down. Sometimes even a simple shift from being in our current mindset is when we recognize what makes us feel confident and powerful and what makes us feel afraid or closed off can make all the difference. When we can we recognize that, we can identify the shift that needs to be made and how we can change it. Which makes us more powerful and more confident.

It can even be a simple shift, like being hunched over, you feel maybe closed off. What's making you feel closed off? Being mindful about that when you go out, you'll start noticing your body language changes, too. You can take that shift and open your arms instead. As soon as you recognize that you do it. Lift up your chest, open your arms, you're warm, you're inviting. Make that shift, and be mindful about it, recognize it. "I just felt afraid, closed off. What made me feel that way? Okay, now I'm going to shut up, move my arms, and lift up my chin again so I feel more confident." When you do that, it will give you that instant boost of confidence. Because you're keeping the heart space open and you're being mindful about it, so you have recognized it, you tackle it, you're changing it, you're making that shift into that confident woman who doesn't need validation. Because you've recognized that, you know your true beauty, and your worth, and you're back to those affirmations of who you are. You have that confidence mindset that actually drives guys wild. Not arrogant, remember, healthy confidence is a huge attraction factor!

So, shift your mindset. Shifting your mindset is empowering, it makes you feel more relaxed because you don't care. You know who you are. It puts you in a state of having fun and being in control of your emotions, you have the power to decide, this is your future.

Here's the thing, and this is a big difference; are you trying to sell yourself on dates? Or are you deciding if this person is worth your time and energy? That's a huge thing. You shouldn't be trying to sell yourself on dates, because that's when people become unauthentic, they aren't completely true to who they are because they're trying to sell some fake version, and that's from a huge lack of self-confidence. Or are you deciding if this person is worth your time and energy? Are they worth being in a relationship with? Write that down and think about that every time you go out. You shouldn't be trying to sell yourself on dates. For example, the woman or man who lies about their age or accomplishments is trying to sell themselves to make the date or a person like them. The confident woman is engaging in conversation to learn if this man is right for her or not, the man is engaging in conversation to see if this woman is right for him. If you are trying to sell yourself to the person, it says you are desperate for someone to like you. Don't be the desperate person, be the confident person to use every situation to your advantage. Because again, confident women don't need validation that they are beautiful or lovable. They already know their true worth and beauty.

Too many people go on dates with one question in the back of their mind, "Will I be liked, accepted, or approved?" And when you're looking for love, you're looking for that soulmate, it's so easy for people to fall into that trap of thinking that the power is in someone else's hands to love and approve of you. That's scary—think about that. They should never have that power.

It does take two people to agree that they want a relationship, but don't forget that you have half the power to decide. It is so important, I want you to remember that. Don't go into a date or social setting with the question, "Will I be liked or accepted or approved of?" Go in with the question of, "Is this person, or are these people, or is this date that I'm meeting worth my time and energy? Are they worth having a relationship with?"

Master your mindset, and that will build confidence. What is the vibe of confidence? Again, it's fun, it's positive, you own the room, you smile, you're friendly, you're warm, you stand tall, you stand open, you are inviting.

Your homework this week is for you to find a place to practice. When you're going out go into a coffee shop or the grocery store, start practicing. Go in, don't cross your arms, smile at people and say, "Hi." Make eye contact. If you see somebody in the same aisle, ask them, "Have you had this ice cream before? What do you think of it?" Try to find a new place to visit, or just make small talk, but find a place to practice confidence. Start with body language, no crossed arms, posture back, arms open, smile, be friendly, eye contact.

Practice with the simple steps, go get your date outfits and then when you walk into a social setting, own the room, walk in with great posture, a smile on your face, be conversational, approach people. You will notice that most people are not interacting and engaging and making the first move, they are waiting for someone else to make the first move. So when you make the first move, you are already ahead of the game. And as I said earlier, men are more attracted to women who will smile and be friendly and approach them and start a conversation than the best looking woman in the room who is standoffish and closed off and looks like she might hit you if you approach her.

Before you go somewhere, you already have affirmations in the back of your mind, make that mindset shift. I want you to go back and review your notes. Make the mindset shifts so when you do find that place to practice, you are ready to go. Also set the affirmations to pop up on your phone, just put them in as a reminder, I do that. I have affirmations pop up throughout the day. Like right now it just popped up. "Today I focus on what I want to attract to my life." I have pictures on my phone screen of; things I want to accomplish. It is a constant reminder.

Then find a place to practice, practice on a friend, practice in your mirror first, create that space of calm before you go out, and then put it into place and be actionable. Don't you dare just take this book and sit behind a computer screen and not put it to work. It doesn't work like that. It's not a like a magic formula. You have to actually put inspired action behind it!

THE POWER OF BODY LANGUAGE

Welcome to Chapter Four. I'm so excited you're here. Now we are going to talk all about the power of body language.

Body language speaks volumes. We talk about communication and saying the right things, but body language actually counts for more communication than the actual words you say, so it's incredibly powerful. The power of body language can be used in your relationships while you're dating, with your friends, or at work, because you can use your body to increase your likability.

I'm going to teach you some key things to use your body language in a positive, classy way. I'm really excited to dig into this. It's really fascinating to me to watch people while they're out on dates, I can usually tell if they're into each other, if it's going to be a one and done type of thing, or if they're irritated with each other. So, once you start recognizing this, you'll start to notice that too, and you can read into your date and play off what they're doing to increase that likability and attraction.

The first thing I want to talk about is to start trying different body language techniques, you have to get in the vibe. You know I talk about this often, but it's so important. You have to shift into the energy of positive body language.

A lot of us have busy days or we're nervous before the date. Work might have been stressful, you might have kids at home and you're trying to get them a babysitter and get to the date, or maybe you're going out with girlfriends and you're wanting to meet new people but you feel like nobody ever approaches you. All these nerves and anxious feelings can add up, and it can really impact our energy and our body language when we're out and about, especially when we're on dates, because we're bringing that energy into our date. So, when we put that tension on us and that nervous energy, it immediately creates a shift in our body language that's not good. So let's shift into that energy of positive body language before you even go out so you already have the foundation, you're already setting yourself up for success.

Before you go out, make sure you take that moment to shift your energy into positive, feminine, flowing, attractive, friendly, warm energy. The kind of energy that people are drawn to, that they want to approach you. Look open and friendly, smile, and be at ease. There's a few ways you can do this. For example, before I was writing the notes for this book, I was just kind of having a hard week. Even though I'm all about high vibes and energy, I have bad days too. I have bad weeks. You're not alone. Even coaches and the people who teach us have bad days, but we know how to shift out of it fast.

I knew I couldn't bring that into this book, so when I was putting the outline together, I knew I had to stop and not put another note in until I shifted that energy because I wanted to bring only good, flowing, positive energy. I didn't want any of that yucky stuff to be attached to my work. This is what I do when I need to shift; I spend the morning praying and meditating. I get a quick workout in. I might even have my own dance party while listening to high vibe music. I'm going to completely shake off the low vibrational energy. And I'm not quoting a Taylor Swift song. I also listen to positive life giving stuff, like podcasts or audiobooks. Another thing that you can do if you're having a bad day or before a date, even if your day isn't that bad and you just want to get past feeling anxious energy, is to do a power pose. If you're not familiar with a power pose, it's when your arms are on your waist, your legs are hip width apart, and you are standing with your chin up, like Superman. The power pose can open up your closed off energy and lift your spirits. Now, I don't recommend doing this when you're on the date or out with friends at a bar because it looks kind of weird, but it's been proven that when you just step into that power pose for a minute, you automatically feel more open, you feel more in control of your feelings and yourself. When you're going to work in the morning, do a power pose before you leave the house, do a power pose before you go on a date. You will start to love the feeling it brings.

So, do something that gets you into that energy shift of something more positive, something more in control of your feelings and emotions. You can meditate, listen to high vibe music, dance, do yoga, work out, take a walk, or power pose it out. Just do what makes you feel good and make that energy shift.

I broke that negative energy that was flowing and welcomed some pretty awesome energy, which I knew I needed for this book and to go about the rest of my day, for my man, for my kids. I needed that positive energy because it impacts my whole family, it impacts my clients, it impacts my approach to life.

Have you ever walked into a room and it felt icky, or felt off? Maybe about someone, the environment or the place? You just felt that negative gray cloud over the place or with that person, and you immediately felt those energy suckers. You walk in and feel the energy being sucked out of you and your good mood suddenly drains out? I know people like that, and I try to stay away from them as much as possible. Just like you can feel the energy of the room people can also feel your energy when you walk in, it's been proven. People will tell me that all the time. When I walk into a room, if I'm in my good energy state, they're like, "Oh, I was drawn to you," or "you have a good energy about you." However, when I'm in my icky energy state, people aren't drawn to me. I see that with other people too. There's people I'm immediately drawn to because their energy is just amazing. I've made friends with some of my clients or I just talked to someone on the phone and we immediately had a connection. I could feel their amazing vibe like you can feel it in someone. So make sure when you go on a date or just out and about (you never know who you will meet!), go in with that high vibe energy. You don't want to go in with low, icky energy that nobody wants to approach.

This is where your body language almost automatically mirrors the vibe you're putting off. Be mindful about this and make that shift before you go out. Have you noticed when you're out and you can see the people who are closed off, they might have their arms crossed, they just have a resting bitch face or you just feel like they don't have good energy. That's exactly the same thing that you want to make sure that you're not doing—be careful that you are an approachable person and that your body language is mirroring that vibe you're putting off.

However, I have a whole meditation bundle on shifting your energy, getting out of that low vibe state, and opening your heart to love—those really good things. It helps you get into that state that you need to be at. The meditations are all about letting go and becoming that high vibe, high match for your soulmate, which is what you're working on. You can get it for free on my website www.datingboutiqueinc.com.

Often, we don't realize we're sending off vibes that repel people instead of attracting them to us. I would say that body language could be one of the number one reason you're in a dating rut right now— you could be scaring people off unintentionally. I think we've all done that at some point. This is so important that you're here today and you're recognizing it. You are going to make the change to make sure that you're more open, that you're actually drawing people in instead of sending them away. You might not be intentionally doing this. I know people who are beautiful, warmhearted people with the best intentions, but their body language is a little off. They look like they don't want to be approached.

Sometimes, when I'm out I like to experiment with body language and see the responses I get. Sometimes I don't smile so I do not get approached or I smile and say hi and then people talk my ear off. I've found there's definitely a difference and I kind of play with it sometimes to see when people approach me and how I act. love to experiment with it, not to get a date, because I have an amazing man but to see how people interact. Remember only a small percentage of what you communicate creates a first impression. The rest is body language, tone and gestures. Only 7% is verbal communication and 93% is body language, voice tone and facial expression. I know we focus so much on what we should say but what really It's all about your body language, your tone of voice, and your facial expressions that create the most engagement. It's not so much about what you say. Just like flirting, only a small percentage is actually the words we say.

That's why it's so important to learn these techniques, so that you can take it out into your dates and when you're out with your girlfriends, work, and wherever it may be. It can be life changing on how much people approach you versus not. When I was researching body language, flirting and all the things that create attraction it was fascinating to learn the importance of the first impression. It's also so interesting to see how men and women are different and how they respond. Women have about fifty-two moves that she might use to show interest, whereas men only have ten. I think that kind of explains us; women are emotional, we're very animated. Men are very simple for the most part.

For example, men might give you the eyebrow flash, when the eyebrow goes up or he leans in more on the date, his feet pointing toward you, that's a huge one. If you're on a date and the man's feet are pointed toward you, that means he's interested. If they're not, it could be that he's nervous, but usually it means he's lost some interest. Don't take it too much to heart. Just pay attention to all of these things so that you can see if he is interested or if he's not. Another sign for men are his legs, if they are spread open a little bit, he's interested. It's like their mating behavior. If he puts his hands in his pockets, with this thumb sticking out, kind of like in a cowboy pose, that means he's interested, he's like trying to man up and win you over, and then the normal things, such as if a man touches the lower part of your back, it's a sign that he's trying to show you he's a protector. Or if he's smiling, it usually means he is interested.

When women are interested in a man she will show her neck more. They'll flip their hair, or maybe touch their collarbone or neck. If she has her head down, and looks up through her eyelashes, think of Marilyn Monroe, it's signs that we might use to show interest, along with laughing and smiling. I bet you don't even realize you're doing these things around a man you're into! It's a subconscious behavior that is ingrained in us to show attraction. And remember, men have about ten, so it's so easy to recognize if he's interested.

I'm going to show you the top body language techniques. How do you use your body language to show interest? Let's get into this. When I say use your body language to show interest, please don't take this as a way to throw yourself at the person. That is not what I mean at all. This is showing your date that you're confident, enthusiastic, fun, warm, friendly, easy to talk to and it's safe to talk to you. That's what this is about. This is not about showing a lot of cleavage. I don't teach that, I don't believe in that. I teach classy is sexy. This is about showing your body in a classy but sexy way that you are interested in the other person.

The first one is eye contact. If a couple has great eye contact going on, they turn toward each other, they're smiling. They're giving each other that really intense eye contact, but it's soft, not glaring and creepy. There's a difference. Keeping eye contact isn't a constant stare, it's maybe glancing down, getting your drink, and then going back to eye contact. Don't look at your phone, don't look around the room or gaze off this shows disinterest. Good eye contact also means you're listening and that you're engaged with them. So, the best way to accomplish this is practice. I know this can be hard, especially when you're nervous and you like someone. You see that cute guy across the room and you make eye contact and you turn away real quick. I used to do that all the time. But you have to maintain it for just a few seconds, get their eye contact, nod slightly, perhaps a soft smile, and then look away. If you are on a date with him and you have maintained eye contact, are listening and engaging in the conversation, then as he's talking and telling a story, glance down to his lips, just softly. You're listening to him talk, maintaining eye contact, and then you glance down and look at his lips and look back up, just kind of in a flirty manner. He sees you look at his lips and look back up. Which says, "I'm interested. I'd love to kiss those lips." He might not register that at that moment, but it is a signal to strengthen attraction.

The second one to note is leaning in, engaging in the conversation. If you're interested in someone, it's important to turn into them and angle your body toward the person instead of away from them. So your feet and shoulders should turn towards that person instead of away from them. Lean in slightly, not too much. Like you're engaged in a conversation or you're interested in what this person is saying. That builds connection. A rule of thumb in this situation is your belly button should be turned toward the person you're interested in. This is another way to gauge if someone's interested in you, if their belly button is turned toward you it is a sign of interest. If it's turned away, it's a sign of lack of interest. I have seen dates where they are sitting side by side, they're not turned in, perhaps at a bar. They're sitting side by side but they're turned away from each other, looking straight ahead. If this is a newly dating couple, perhaps a first date, this is a huge red flag; nobody is interested. But if they're turned towards each other, then you know they're interested. You can tell they're not engaging if their feet are turned away from each other and there's also more space between them. If someone's sitting closer to you, maybe their knee or their leg is gently grazing yours, or there's not much space between you and you turn toward each other in some form, then there's more interest there. If you want to repel somebody, then do this; don't be engaged, turn your feet away from them, and look straight ahead and create space. For example, me and my husband, when we first started dating, I remember I started watching his body language, and he turned toward me, he created very little space between us when we were sitting, and he leaned in during the conversation, his arms were open, all those things that show that someone's interested in you. You are trying to create that interest, because you can also do these things to help open them up as well. Even if they're not doing them at first, you can do it to create more interest and attraction there. Remember open body language can create more attraction.

The third one to note is how to mirror a vibe, which is very interesting. You can even do this when you're at a business dinner or networking event to create more attraction. This technique will make people want to hang out with you, want to talk with you, and want to network with you. Here's the trick, you have to learn how to mirror and understand someone else's vibe. It is so important that you learn this because to relate to others effectively, you need to be able to read the other person. So, what does mirroring someone else do? It actually activates your date's brain to prompt them to be more open, it makes you look more attractive. That's the secret here: mimicking them means imitating someone's body language, which establishes rapport and gets them to trust you. It sends a subconscious signal that you two are alike, you have commonalities, you're the same. Make sure it's natural and not obvious, don't copy them immediately. Wait a second. Iif they have their arms crossed, I wouldn't do that. Don't mimic negative body language, but mimic the positive body language. If they're leaned in or they're sitting in an open, inviting manner, when you mimic them it will create that subconscious connection and build attraction for you. And automatically, this is one of the strongest techniques of body language that you can use for your benefit.

The next one is touch. Touch is part of body language and can be flirty, gentle and not over the top. For example, gently touching on the arm, hand or knee. A great place to get a guy is to touch the area between his wrist and his mid arm just a few times during the night, gently but flirty. For men, they will gently touch her lower back to guide her, to show that they're there to protect her and be that man. Make sure it's gentle and not grabbing his arms. Just very gentle and flirty. When I was dating, I had people do creepy stuff sometimes. So, obviously, I didn't go on another date with them. But don't intently grab their hand to hold it.. That's just over the top. If you're on a first date, you're not in love. Don't do that, that's scary and creepy. Don't grab and hang on to their hands or their arms.

And finally, the obvious—smile, smile often. A lot of people don't do this. Resting bitch face kills the connection, I promise, it does. There's sayings out there like "Being a bitch, win the man" or "Nice girls, finished last." No, that is not true. I've worked with 1000s of men and that is not true. If they do end up marrying those people, it's built on a false, unauthentic basis. And they usually don't last. If you want to remain single or perpetually in the wrong relationships listen to the advice of being a bitch or playing games to get the guy. If you want to have a ring on your finger with a genuine high quality man listen to my advice. I'm telling you authenticity works. Resting bitchface kills connection, so smile. You have to be friendly, be inviting, where he wants to open up to you, where he wants to talk to you. This shows you're interested and engaged. You might touch your neck gently while you're at the table, that builds attraction, it shows you're sexy but classy. Or tilt your head and slightly look down, give a gentle bat of your eyelashes, but not over the top where it looks awkward. You can practice in the mirror. Although sometimes we might even catch yourself doing this naturally. These are ways that you can tell when there is interest, and make sure that you show interest as well.

How to know when it's fake or real? I think we've all seen those people who put on a face. They fake happiness, give a fake smile, but there are some key things that can show inauthenticity. You probably recognize the people who give the fake smile. Maybe it's on a date, they're just getting through just to be polite or whatever it may be. You might have done it too with a date, the fake smile, the fake engagement, whatever it may be. But you can tell if it's fake or real. Is it a smile that looks forced? Or is it a smile that says, "I'm engaged in this conversation." Another way is to note if the lips are pursed but open. If they purse their lips, they are holding back something they may want to say, they're not going to say it because they don't feel like they can, they're not going to be open with you. To see if it's real or fake engagement, if they're leaning in, having fun, smiling, laughing, arms are open, it's real, they're really trying to engage with you and create that interest. If they are leaned back, arms crossed, feet pointed away, the smile doesn't reach their eyes, then they are not engaged.

Another little trick is to stand in the middle of the group, because everybody is naturally drawn to look at what is in the middle. When you're out and you see a group of people, our eyes are naturally going to whoever's in the middle. So if you're with a group of friends and you're trying to get people to approach you, it's advisable to stand in the middle. If you're sitting at a table, sit in the middle.

Dale Carnegie said, "It's easier to make friends when you show interest in them instead of trying to get them interested in you." And I think this is a powerful quote, because oftentimes, we go on dates and we want this person to be interested in us. Instead of showing interest in them, we might talk all about the good things about us, like how great we are and keep ourselves as the center of discussion in an attempt to make us look good. The fact is, that is actually going to do the opposite. It's easier to make friends, to get that date, to get someone to approach you, or get that second, third, fourth date, that long term relationship when you show more interest in them instead of trying to get them interested in you. So that means acting more engaged and leaning in, laughing and having fun, asking a lot of questions about them to get to know them. Ask open ended questions. And then return the question with your answer with more about you. This creates a conversation that flows and it doesn't make it feel like an interview of questions about them.

A lot of times women will tell you, "Well, he didn't ask me a lot of questions about myself, he seemed kind of self-absorbed." But that's not always the case, that's not always true. He might have been nervous. And he might not know how to ask good questions. What I've found in over a decade of studying communication - most people don't have great communication skills especially when they're nervous. So it's important for you to open that line of communication, to ask questions, and be prepared with a list of top ten questions to keep the conversation going.

Remember, it's easier for them to become interested in you when you act interested in them first, and that's huge when it comes to dating. That's how you can build that attraction and get that second, third, or forever date. This is because you're showing them interest, you're engaged, and you're creating connection.

When my husband and I were on our first date, I actually only planned on meeting him for an hour. I promised myself I would only spend an hour or so on a first date to get to know them and then go from there. And that particular night I was going to go meet friends after the date. Well our date ended up being over four hours. But he later told me, "That was one of the best dates I've had." And all we did was talk, because I showed interest in him. I asked a lot of questions, and I was engaged in getting to know him. It did help that he was incredibly handsome when he walked in. Not that I thought this was 'the one' at that moment. But I thought I like this guy, he could be fun, even as a friend, and I wanted to get to know him because I could see myself hanging out with him, even if it didn't end up in a romantic relationship. It is so important to ask questions, show interest, and that's how you can potentially find your one.

Now let's talk about putting all of this together and making the magic happen. How do we create that magic flirting formula to find and keep our high quality man? Practice, practice, practice—all kinds of practice!

You have to put the knowledge into place, you have to be proactive about it or it's not going to happen, and it's not going to happen overnight; you have to practice it. Body language is something that we've been using since we were kids and the same body language is probably still ingrained in us. So we have to make those changes to make a new habit and practice good body language. It's really important to start being mindful as you go out and what you're doing, what kind of body language you're putting out there. The thing is, everyone can improve their daily life and become mindful of the vibe, the body language, and the communication skills that they put out there. Everyone can do it, but a lot of people don't. So when we become self-aware of our body language, our flirting techniques, and how we engage in a conversation, we can become powerful, high vibe, women. Absolutely powerful.

With my coaching clients, I put a lot of these things into place with them from the beginning. And by the second coaching session, they've already found somebody new to date. It's like clockwork' they're already out there, finding people, and they're getting in exclusive relationships faster. So you can do this too. I wasn't named one of the top dating coaches in the world for no reason (a little shameless plug). You can start practicing these things and become that incredible high-vibe single. Everybody can do it. Remember, it's about becoming mindful of your vibe, your body language, and your communication skills that you put out there. Put in all those flirting techniques and engage in conversation and you will be a powerhouse.

When we begin to master these human connection techniques, we immediately become more attractive. When you do this, you'll start to see the difference, but you have to practice and make mindful decisions each step of the way. And make it a habit, because it's going to be hard sometimes, we're so used to responding in certain ways. But when you make this a habit and you put these human connection techniques into place, you will become more attractive automatically. That means you attract higher quality dates, it's a fact.

So even if you're not doing it naturally right now, you can fake it until you make it. It's not that you're being inauthentic, it's that you're practicing, you're trying to set the foundation for a better mindset, a better dating life, a better way of engaging with people. Just simply fake it until you make it in that way. If you lack confidence, you need to continue to practice that positive body language every day. Because over time, it will become natural, and it will increase your confidence. I promise you that. Make it actionable. Get out there and practice positive body language throughout the week while you're at work, while you're out with friends, or on the next date, while at the grocery store, the coffee shop, everywhere you go—practice!

Remember, if you're in the habit of creating or having that normal body language that you have now, what you've grown up with, now is the time to create a new norm. And I promise if you start putting these skills into action and recognizing others' body language, your dating life will improve.

So, get out there this week. Put it all into action every single day, make a note on your phone, in your calendar, and get to work. And drop me some emails to let me know how it goes. I love you guys. I'll see you in the next chapter.

CHAPTER FIVE

COMMUNICATION - MASTER THE OPENING LINE

So, we are on Chapter four, and you're almost done with *The Art of Flirting* book. I am so excited for you, I'm so proud. I know the people who make the investment and take the time to create a better dating life and healthier relationships are the ones who succeed. Those are the people who end up with a high value relationship or dating life. And it's just so exciting to see someone's progress, how their relationships improve and how much their dating life improves. Here's the thing, not many people actually take the time to really invest in themselves, and you have already done that, you're doing that right now. You're taking the time for that.

Today's Chapter is all about communication. It's about mastering the opening line and mastering communication, because we can use communication to build attraction. I think the most important thing to take away from this is that you can use these tools and these skills to build attraction on dates and create that opportunity for people to want to ask you out on the second, third, fourth, fifth date. And eventually your last date with them, which would be the forever date. So, use these tools to build attraction.

Communication is the number one key to a long-term, successful, healthy relationship. A lot of people who have been married fifty years, twenty years, whatever it may be, the number one thing that they practice is they have a really great foundation of communication. So this is a skill, this is something that people have to learn and build on. It doesn't always come naturally, and that's okay. Learn to be patient with yourself as you strengthen and work on your communication skills, because it doesn't come overnight all the time. We are not always born with great communication skills, it takes work and practice.

Oftentimes, our communication skills have been impacted by our childhood, our past relationships, which have created not so healthy communication skills, and it's okay, it's just that we need to recognize how we can improve this and make those changes. Life is a series of growth. We all have areas of improvement to grow into the highest version of ourselves and we have to start somewhere within each area. If your dating life is lacking then start recognizing the areas of growth needed to get you to the place you desire. I don't believe anyone is 100% perfect in their relationships but the ones that succeed look for opportunities of growth and take inspired action to get to the place they desire.

For me, just a little background, I had horrible communication skills. Growing up in my household was very toxic, the communication was not open, I wasn't really allowed to have a voice, and there was no open dialogue. It was 'my way or the highway' type of communication with my parents. I didn't have much communication with my biological father. We did have a relationship, but it wasn't a great one. I never learned how to successfully communicate, and I was a very shy child in elementary school. Eventually, I started to break out of that and I actually went back to college to study communication. My degree is in Communication with a focus in interpersonal and intimate communication. I purposely chose to study and focus on interpersonal and intimate communication because I knew that's where I struggled. I wanted to be able to teach people how to create those long-term, healthy, relationships, but at first I had to teach myself.

The point is, anybody can learn these skills, especially if I can learn them, because I had horrible communication skills. Today, the relationship I'm in, we have great communication, but it also takes work to continue on a path of growth. I told you guys a story earlier about when we had our first date, I planned on staying for an hour and we ended up talking for four hours. And he told me that that was one of the best dates, because of the conversation. We have stayed like that since that first date. When we were dating, and before we were living together, we would talk every day on the phone for an hour. We would talk about everything, from the stupidest things to the most serious, and we still do that today. If you can build the skill, it's totally possible, and I'm not saying you have to talk to the person you're dating for an hour every day, that was just something that we did.

Communication is the number one key to build a long term healthy relationships. I'm going to take you through how to create that good dialogue, to create that flowing conversation, but you can also use these skills to take into your future relationship.

The thing about communication is that the lack of communication creates misunderstanding, and authentic relationships grow when there's open communication. It is important that you can tell what you need in a relationship, who you really are, what you are feeling, and all those things in between. When we have a lack of communication and we don't create that openness, this is when we create misunderstanding in relationships. It can fail and not go to the next level or you might not get that second, third, fourth, fifth date. Therefore, it's very important to learn this skill, so that there's no misunderstanding when you are dating and building those relationships. Instead you're building a relationship that flourishes.

Creating an open and safe environment of communication is a must in any relationship. I know many of us have experienced rejection. And we might have that fear of rejection if we're open in our conversation, if we are completely open and authentic, we might fear that we'll be rejected for what we say or how they perceive us, and that is totally normal. However, the thing is the person who rejects you for being a hundred percent yourself, is not your person and is not meant to have a place in your story. Remember that when you're on a date—be open, be who you are, because you want to be with that person who wants to be with you for who you are, not a false version of yourself. And I know it can be hard, but practice on creating that open, safe communication, even from the beginning stages of a relationship. Now, I'm not saying go share everything, just share sprinkles of yourself throughout the dating relationship. And be open about it. Don't make up anything, don't say anything that's false, but just create an open, safe place to have that conversation flowing authentically.

One of my pet peeves in the dating space is when people play dating games. For example, they might wait two days to respond to a message, play hard to get or they lie about their age. Those people are so unauthentic, and they set up a foundation of a toxic relationship. When people are open and authentic, they create healthier relationships and they attract healthier people. But then we start to play games, we start to include lies that can snowball into a very unhealthy dating relationship), such as lying about your age or smoking or your height, which I see all the time, especially with men, they say they're six foot on the online dating profile and you get there and they're 5'10, or women who lie about their age, they say they're thirty and they're really thirty-five. Even if you look younger, don't lie, somebody is going to find out. Stay authentic. Also, remember; what you put out there is who you attract. If you're putting out all these dating games and not being authentic, trying to talk yourself up to this other person, you are actually going to attract someone who does the same thing. And then you're new relationship is based on lies. Wouldn't you get mad if you found out that person lied to you? Of course, you would. So why set that up from the beginning? Be completely open and authentic with your dates. This will actually build attraction too.

There are two types of communication. There's verbal and non-verbal, and we talked about this a little bit in the other chapters. Non-verbal is body language, flirting, tone of voice and then verbal is the actual communication. Each one is equally important and needs to be mastered, because when you put it all together, it helps you create that atmosphere of success. However, we are talking in this chapter about verbal communication. Use this chapter with the chapter on body language and all the flirting techniques. The verbal only plays a small part in the whole picture of getting a date's attention but it plays a crucial role in keeping the relationship going long term.

The next part focuses on how to keep the conversation flowing and how to start the conversation. It is important to focus on being curious about the other person, ask a lot of questions about the person, the more you look interested in that person, instead of focusing on being the interesting person, the more attraction levels grow. Be the curious person, show your interest, and keep that conversation flowing in a give and take type of way.

I'm going to give you some tips on how to keep that conversation flowing, how to ask questions, what not to ask, what not to do, and really build that engagement up. I encourage you to use it when you're messaging back and forth with online dating, but also reference it after you've been dating for months or when you're in a serious relationship. It is important to really focus on this on your first dates. This will keep that interaction going, keep the person wanting more, and get that second and third date.

The first thing to do is to ask engaging questions. Don't just talk about yourself, ask about the other person and think of topics ahead of time. Do some research before you go on dates. Google some interesting topics that are going on in the world, or learn a new hobby, find out something interesting, some new facts about a destination you want to go to or that you've gone to. There's so many things to learn about in this world. Think of some fun, interesting topics ahead of time, and keep it engaging. Don't just talk about yourself, make sure you're asking about the other person more than talking about yourself.

The second thing to note is a way to start conversations. You could ask about their favorite things. Don't do it in an interview tone where it sounds boring and bland. "What's your favorite music? Sports? Food?" I hear this too often that people felt like they were on an interview with their date because the date asked all those interview questions like you're on a job, "So, how old are you? What job do you have? How many siblings do you have? What do you like to do on the weekends?" Very straightforward without any personality behind the conversation, and there's not enough engagement questions. They didn't know how to turn those questions into something fun. Which you can do—turn questions into something fun. For instance, you could ask, "What type of music do you love?" And then after they answer, they ask "What type of music do you love?" and then after you tell them what you love, say, "Okay, what's the most unlikely concert that you've ever been to?" And then they give their answer. And there might be a funny story behind that, like, "Oh, my gosh, I can't believe you went to that concert! You have to tell me the story of how you ended up at a concert like that!" And then you can tell them your most unlikely concert, or what was the first concert that you ever went to? And you can do the same thing with food, you can ask "Okay, so what's the most unlikely food you've ever tried?" Then you tell them what you've tried and maybe you have a really fun travel story to go with it. And then you can do that with every question. You can tie those answers to a story. It could be an embarrassing, hilarious, or funny story, travel stories are the best. So if you travel a lot, you probably have a lot of stories to share about your different experiences. And if you don't travel, just get out into your community and start exploring, because you'll meet new people and you'll create new experiences to share about the city. And you can tie those in to these basic questions to make the conversation more engaging, more fun. You learn more about that person and they learn more about you. So it's not boring. It's important to take those questions to another level, to another question, to keep that engagement going. Not talking about one subject the whole conversation, but you can turn it into like two or three more questions to really learn more about this person's interest. I still do this with my husband today. For example, a certain song came on the radio that reminded me of the time I was invited to that musician's birthday party. I turned to my husband and said, "Did I ever tell you about the time I was invited to their birthday party?" He was like "What!?!" Don't get me wrong, sometimes our conversations are completely dull but it's important to keep the interesting stories and conversations going throughout your relationship. I even have conversation starters saved to ask him while we're on roadtrips. I want to constantly be learning about my partner and I want him to know I'm still interested in him years later. Just a little tidbit on how to keep that spark and curiosity flowing throughout your relationship.

Third thing to note is not to tell your life story. One of the parts of our business as we look at online dating profiles and do makeovers on them, is we notice a lot that people like to put their whole life story in their online dating profile. Don't do that. You're giving away the whole farm, you should sprinkle in information about yourself and keep it short and simple. You want people to be curious about you and want to learn more about you, not already have all the information or they think they have all the information and then base a decision of not contacting you because they think, "Okay, I already know everything about this person, it doesn't interest me." You want to get them curious and get them to ask questions and to go on that date. So, don't tell your whole life story on your online dating profile. Don't tell it on your dates, sprinkle in information about yourself along the way to get them asking questions and to get them curious to learn more and wait to see you again.

Another important thing is to never talk about your past exes or your past dates. Reveal just a little bit about that stuff at a time, and save that for like date five, date six. Save the past baggage conversations for later, that can be viewed as drama. And drama is a big turnoff! I think it's funny to ask, for example, if you go on an online date or you meet someone that you met online and you can be like, "Okay, so tell me your worst online dating experience," because everybody's had one, and they're usually pretty hilarious. That's funny not drama. I'm talking about past relationships that left you heartbroken or a crazy ex story. Keep the drama stories for another time. The first date should always be light and fun. Remember that you want to be authentic but at the same time not scare them away right up front. Because when we start talking about our past relationships, sometimes it can scare people away.

The next one is to stay away from conversations such as politics, religion, marriage, all that stuff. These can be hot topics with very major differences in opinion for each person. And it can cause heated conversations. This is something you want to stay away from on your first date. Because the first day is meant to be just easy breezy, light and fun, not so serious. Serious discussions should be left for later dates and not brought up early on. You might want to date someone who has the same religious beliefs as you, but usually you already know that, especially if you're dating online, they'll usually have their religious preferences. So there's no need to bring it up on the first date or the second date. Also, stay away from topics like marriage and kids. If you go on the date and you're like "Well, I want to get married within five years and have two kids" and blah, blah, blah, blah. That will leave the man running and he probably will not call you again! Even though he might want that eventually, don't bring that up on the first date. He might think you're just out to get married and get a ring on your finger.

Remember, a good thing about this is to remember to accept that this person is not you and they will have their own perspectives or thoughts, their own feelings and their own life experiences around these subjects. So, just accept that we all have different opinions and feelings about these things.

The fifth point is to be authentic and truthful. This is so important, and I don't understand why people use these little white lies on their dates to try to get people to like them better. Because eventually they will find out, and this can seriously bite you in the butt in the future if you ever tell a lie. Never ever tell a lie, let's say you end up on like date ten and you fudge about your success or your age. But now things are getting serious, and if you lied, then you take a huge risk of that person eventually finding out one way or another and possibly a great relationship ending because you wanted to tell some white lie in the beginning, which is ridiculous. Why would you risk ending that relationship because of some stupid white lie?

You want someone who wants you for who you are, not some fake person you put on before. Being dishonest means you've already created a toxic foundation, and that's just setting a relationship up for failure automatically. So make sure you're open, truthful, and authentic at all times.

The sixth point is to be curious about their job, have questions. "Wow that sounds interesting. How did you get into that? What do you see yourself doing in the future?" But stay away from the money talk. It's not your business how much they make. It makes you sound bad if you ask that question, like you're focused on money and not actually interested in them as a person. The money conversation can come up later down the road if you both become exclusive and you're headed that way into a serious relationship. But, the money conversations should not come up during the initial dating period. And it is a turn off when women ask men how much they make.

The seventh point is don't ask about the next date. Let him lead. When you're done with a date. Don't ask, "Okay, so when are we going to see each other again?" Let him lead. Instead say, "I had a great time tonight, thank you for the drink and dinner," and then let him ask for that second date. Now, once you've had a few dates, you can say, "Hey, would you like to go here?" Maybe you have tickets to a game or you have this great hiking adventure going on. You could ask him that.

The eighth point is to stay away from negativity and drama. I think this is a well-known thing, but people still do it. So don't talk about negative things like how bad your day was and how bad your job is and how bad your sister is. All those things or any past drama, drama that's going on with your friends, stay away from that, especially if you're in the first stages of dating, this could scare someone away. This tells a guy whoa this girl is a handful and I'll be sucked into to all her drama. Most men hate drama and will run from women that follow it. Also, don't put yourself down. The lack of self-confidence is a major turnoff. Self confidence is attractive. I'm not saying to have over the top self-confidence, like you can't stop talking about yourself and your achievements. It's when you're just confident in who you are as a person, you don't put yourself down, you're proud of who you are, you're comfortable in your own skin. Those are the things that are attractive. Just don't put yourself down on the date. It will scare people off. High quality men don't like to hang around women that are full of pity parties and doom and gloom.

Now, here are eleven conversation starters to help engage more within each question. On some conversation starters you'll see a main question and then a sub question to create more engagement. For example, you will see the first question, "Where's considered home?" So you can ask, but then show interest. Don't just ask the question and then not engage with the question. So you could ask, "Where's considered home?" And then you can ask, so, "What was it like living there? Does your family still live there? What's your favorite memory of your childhood?" Don't ask it back to back, let him answer and then grab something that he says and ask another question. I'm not saying make the whole conversation or whole night about this one subject, but enough that you can learn about him and you're showing you're interested, you're engaging in a conversation and really pulling information from him and giving him information in return. Don't just ask questions without giving answers back. If he said his home is considered Michigan, you could say, "Oh, my home is considered Kentucky," or whatever it may be, "What was it like living there?" And then you can go back and forth.

Bonus Conversation Starters

I've included 11 questions to start a conversation and engage more within each question. On some conversation starters you'll see a main question and then a sub question to create more engagement.

1. Where is considered "home"?

    - Where were you raised?
    - What was it like living there?
    - Does your family still live there?
    - What's your favorite memory?

2. Who is the most important person in your life?

    - How did they influence you?
    - How did you meet?

3. What's your average weekend look like? Saturday morning priorities: sleep, exercise, or aggressive mimosa?

    - What's your favorite things to do?
    - If you could have the perfect weekend what would that look like?

4. What are you passionate about?

    - How did you get into that?
    - What are your goals with your passion?

5. What's your biggest dream?

  - Why would you like to accomplish that?
  - Show interest and curiosity

6. What was your first job? (Great question after you ask about their career.)

  - Did you like it? Why or why not?
  - What was the best thing about the job?

7. If you're at a restaurant or bar ask "What is your go to drink?"

8. What's the best meal you've ever had?

9. What's your favorite tv show? Movie?

10. What would be your super power if you could have one?

11. What's on your bucket list?

  - Have you completed anything on your bucket list?

In these eleven prompts provided, you can really dig into them and get those conversations flowing. You could also use the more simple ones, to create that conversation online if you're online dating. So what you can do, for example on Bumble, where the woman has to initiate the conversation, you could say, "Saturday morning priorities, sleep, exercise, or aggressive mimosas?" And then, he'll answer and you can respond as well. A little secret, that's the first question I asked my husband when we matched online. His answer was perfect and I knew I would have fun hanging out with him. And the rest is history! Or you can say, "If you could have a perfect weekend? What would it look like?" Don't ask all these back to back, but just kind of let it flow and allow a give and take. Ask a lot of questions, give some answers, pull out some more information, give some answers. And let it flow back and forth. The eleven different topics can create a really good flow of conversation.

Next, practice positive bids. So, what is a bid you may ask? I absolutely love this practice. I learned this when I was in college, as I studied Dr. John Gottman, a relationship expert. He is amazing, his work just fascinates me. A bid comes from one of his books called *The Relationship Cure*. And I highly recommend it - just go to my website, Datingboutiqueinc.com and click on Amanda's Favorite Things in the upper menu, and you'll see a list of books that I absolutely love and recommend. I highly recommend this practice, because it really determines the success of a relationship in the early stages to when you've been married for years.

Positive bids are simply responding positively when your dating partner says or does something. For example, you could be recognizing their accomplishments. If they accomplish something at work, you recognize it and say, "Oh, I'm so proud of you. That's amazing." Or by simply recognizing your partner and listening with interest. It could be something like responding to simple requests. "Hey, babe, will you go get the mail for me? Will you pick up a latte from the coffee shop?" Or even little requests. "Will you help me clean off the table?" And you respond in a positive manner. Those are positive bids, or when you show interest and excitement in the conversation. Showing interest, showing excitement, being engaged in the conversation, you turn toward them and you show you're engaged. It's as simple as responding to a joke your partner tells you. There's nothing worse than when a guy tells a joke and the girl doesn't respond, that's a negative bid, and it kind of crushes them. To give your partner a positive bid, answer questions, and pay attention to him. Giving affection, turning toward someone to give them eye contact and acknowledgement, that's a positive bid.

Now, a negative bid is when you don't respond to them and ignore them. There's no affection, there's no signs of interest. Those are all negative bids. And it's proven that our relationship needs five positive bids for every negative bid to survive. So I encourage you to learn more about this, and read the book *The Relationship Cure* by Dr. John Gottman. You can use this practice in your dating life early on and create the habit of positive bids to set up your future relationship for success.

When you date to build attraction, you can actually do this to create that connection and make them want to see you again. So practice giving positive bids. You can practice these on your friends or your family so that you can get into the habit of doing them and the difference they make, because sometimes we don't even realize that we are giving a negative bid, such as ignoring someone, and that can really hurt a relationship, any type of relationship.

The next thing we're going to do is make it actionable; you have to get out there and make it happen. If you don't actually put this to work, it's not going to work for you. You can listen to this or read this till you're blue in the face, but it's not going to work unless you go out there and actually do it. So, with each chapter, I want you to practice its topic focus. Please get out there and do something to put these into place. Because once you start doing that, you'll start to notice the difference, your confidence will rise and you'll be a powerhouse.

Remember the bonus tip questions are with this chapter. Memorize some of those. And then I want you to get out and start practicing with your friends and your family and put it into action on dates. It takes twenty-one days for something to become a habit. This is something you need to combine. So, flirting techniques and styles, communication, body language; all that needs to be practiced daily so that it becomes a habit. And then when you start going on dates, you're automatically doing it without thinking about it. It just flows so naturally, it'll be amazing. Even with online dating, you can take some of these and put it into action. But don't just sit behind a computer screen and message someone back and forth forever with these questions. These are actually meant to create connections with people in person. Message back and forth for a day or two, max a week, move to that in-person date as quickly as possible so you're not wasting time as a pen pal.

The thing is, text messaging, online dating and social media, all that is great. But you can't experience that full connection without being right next to someone and hearing the emotion behind their voice, seeing how they interact and experiencing their personality. It's just a whole different experience. You can't create connections just by being online. You have to actually get out and meet in person to make that amazing connection happen.

So get out from behind that computer screen. Go to a coffee shop, go somewhere, just start to put these things into action immediately so that you can succeed and master all these tips. Pretty soon, you'll do it without even thinking twice.

CHAPTER SIX

PUT IT INTO ACTION, BECOME IRRESISTIBLE, AND LAND THE DATE!

I am so excited. I am so proud of you. The thing is, you guys took the initiative, you are taking the chance at finding love, you are doing the work. It's when people do the work that miracles happen. And it's like that every single time. Because if we just sit there and we expect it to happen, that's when things become stagnant, there's no massive action taking place, and you aren't creating the atmosphere for those miracles to come into your life.

I was actually just talking to a producer today, I'm doing a little project, and we were talking about how people don't prepare for success in their dating life. They also don't prepare their mindset, they don't prepare their physical health, or the wellness of their body to bring that high quality partner into their life. And when you want to prepare for good things or you want good things to come into your life, you have to prepare. It's just like going to school—you prepare with a degree to get your dream job. If you want to lose weight, you have to dedicate yourself to eating healthy and exercising, just like if you want to prepare for your soulmate, you have to do the work behind it. You have to mentally, physically, and emotionally prepare and heal.

My point with that is that you have done that; you've started doing the work. So you are going to start seeing differences in how you interact with people. The type of people that you date will be different, because you're leveling up. When we level up in any area of our life amazing things happen, it's like clockwork. I'm getting stories from people who are doing the exact work I put in this book, and they're going out and they're changing their body language, they're meeting and connecting with people in ways they never connected before. It's amazing, and that will happen for you if you put it to work.

Now that you have learned about the science behind flirting, if you can really play with what you learned when you're out, you also learned about confidence, the power of body language and communication. What I want you guys to do with this chapter is put everything into action. Because if you just leave it here and leave it stagnant, you are not going to see the change, you have to actually take massive action to create success. And that's with anything in life. So my goal for you right now at the end of this book is for you to create massive action.

The weekend is coming, now is the time to put this to work. The more you do it, the better you'll get, I promise. I know, it might be getting out of your comfort zone, but that's the whole purpose of this book. It was to get you out of your comfort zone.

I want to talk about how to put it all into action. You learned a lot, there's a lot that you can put into place. Where do you start? Well, you start somewhere small. What I suggest is making a note on your phone and saying, "I'm going to try the body language techniques the next time I go out," and just start there. Then, try the communication techniques. And then you can combine them a little bit here and there. And after a while, those will just start to come naturally, and it won't feel so awkward. The more you practice something, the more it becomes a habit, and that's when it starts to become natural.

In essence, we can pick up things that we don't even notice, and we can carry it into our adult life. These things are capable of affecting our relationships. Sometimes I noticed with my husband when he was talking I would have my arms crossed. And he was like, "Well, can you please stop crossing your arms when we're having a discussion because it makes you look standoffish." And I said, "You're so right." I didn't realize I was doing that, but it does make me appear more standoffish. It's something you have to learn, and you have to adjust. Now when I'm talking to him and we're having a serious discussion, I'm more mindful about keeping my arms open and keeping that space open. I'm more inviting, welcoming, and I'm not putting him off.

We have to be mindful about these everyday things that we might not notice that we do but may be affecting our relationship. We can make those small adjustments here and there. Of course, it's not going to happen overnight. Don't beat yourself up. Just make those small adjustments so that you become more open and confident when you walk in the room like you own the place.

What I want to focus on is what we can do to let it flow and let it come with ease. I want you ladies to create some affirmations that declare the best version of yourself , write down what you want to accomplish. For example, "I walk into the room with ease," "I walk into the room with confidence," "I walk into the room and own the place." What is your affirmation? What do you want to accomplish? Do you want that confidence? Do you want it to be, "I can flirt with anybody with confidence, I am open, I am at ease, I can create healthy, amazing conversations with my dates. I am friendly, I am inviting, they want to date me, they want to see me again"? Whatever that affirmation is, you can play with it as much as you want, you can create twenty-five, you can create a hundred, you can create one, whatever you want to do. I want you to take some affirmations and I want you to create them based on this book and what you want to accomplish. I want you to plug it into your phone right now as a reminder so that it pops up every single day until it happens. It is so important. We are always wanting to become the best version of ourselves. So to do that we have to focus on what we want to become now. What do we want to accomplish? Do we want that soulmate? Then how are we going to get there? How are we going to become the best version of ourselves so that we attract that best version date? We have to be who we want to attract. And walk as if you are acting as the highest version of yourself.

So get your journal out, create at least five affirmations, and then put those into your phone, put them in your journal, you can put them on post it notes around your house, I still have one on my mirror and I change it out every day. The one on my mirror says "what would the highest version of myself do?" And that just reminds me, not just in my relationships with my family, my loved ones, but with my business and with my wellness goals, my business goals, my relationship goals, what would the highest version of myself do? How would I relate to this person? What would I do in my business? Would I work out every day? Yes. Would I eat more healthy? Yes. Would I communicate better? Yes. Would I spend more quality time with the people I love? Yes. I always asked myself that question, and it helps keep me on track. But you can do that with absolutely any affirmation, it helps you to become accountable.

Here's the thing when it comes to relationships, attracting that high-value man, and dating successfully, it's all about ease and flow. When you are out with your girlfriends, you see some hottie and you're afraid to approach him or when he does approach you you shrink back. When we communicate, we have to do it with a sense of ease and flow. So there's no tension. It should come easy, there's no need for it to be complicated or difficult. And oftentimes, we want to put some type of control on a situation and the outcome. But we have to let it flow with ease and release that control, release the "How," of How it's going to happen when we meet our soulmate. Release the "How" of what's going to happen next with the inter-action with this person. Because if this person is not your person, then there's no need to control that situation for them to stay, that can really backfire. Release control, approach the date with ease.

Let's say you're on a first date, go with the mindset of "this could be my person or it could not, but I'm in the process of finding the love of my life, and this is just a step in that direction." That releases the control, fear, and anxiety. It's just a meeting, and you're in the process of finding the love of your life. Same thing when you go out with your friends; you're in the process, you're having fun, you're enjoying yourself, you're at ease. You're letting the interactions flow. But we should not put so much control over, "I'm going to meet somebody tonight." Well, your person might not be there tonight. If you're making the effort, you're taking the steps, you're putting in the work to prepare yourself to meet your person, it's just a matter of time. We have to trust the process, even when it looks hopeless and difficult. There's just a refining process to get us to where we need to be. Release that control, release the how of how it's going to happen, don't get so caught up in all of that, because that just creates anxiety. And when we try to create control of a situation, it doesn't end up well. It just doesn't. It's when we let go, we are at ease, we are having fun, and we are enjoying life that what's meant to be becomes a magnet to us. Just lean back into creating that amazing life, that amazing situation where you can flirt and have fun. He might not be your person, but you can still enjoy yourself. Don't get tensed up about what could happen about that, the end result, just have fun with it.

That's an affirmation, you should say or you should write down—it's all easy. It's easy. It flows. "Love flows to me, I let go of the outcome, I let go of the "How" my soulmate is on his way to me right now, I'm enjoying the process. I'm enjoying the process. I'm overflowing with joy and love. My dating life is successful. My dating life is amazing. My soulmate is on his way to me right now. I am ready for him. I am preparing. I'm becoming the best version of myself so that I can be the wife of his dreams. He is on his way to me."

What if we changed our mindset? Instead of focusing on finding someone and being focused on finding that soulmate, we just let go, we know it's going to happen. We've done the work, we're doing the work every day, we are walking as the best version of ourselves. What if our number one attention when we went out was just to have fun and feel good? What if we switch that and from that neediness of trying to find someone to, "I feel good. I feel amazing, I'm going to have fun. That's my intention when I go out." It's not so much trying to seek and find your soulmate but more like "I love me, I'm having fun, I'm going to enjoy myself. I'm living life to the fullest as the highest version of myself" That's when things start to happen, when we switch those intentions. And we start to become mindful of just having fun while we are out, we immediately become more attractive and people are drawn to us, because we are laughing, we're having fun, we're enjoying ourselves. That is powerful in itself. How would you think that would change the interaction you have with this person? It would completely change it. They would think, "Oh, wow, they're confident, they're having fun. They're so easy to talk to you. I want to see them again." That's what happens when you switch that intention.

So you do the work and then trust the process. I want you to get in that state of overflowing ease, overflowing in your personal life, overflowing in your dating life. If one date goes bad, there's always another date out there that will go better, and eventually lead you to your forever date. So just think of dating as a sense of overflow. You have enough, there's enough men out there, there's so many good men, you're in a state of overflow, you're going to find your person. So don't push it.

Questions people have asked me about flirting:

"I can't get the courage to approach someone, what do I do?"

That's okay, courage is practiced. You're just getting started, so it will take longer to get out of your comfort zone. Don't beat yourself up, do the small steps, it could be approaching someone that you don't even find attractive and starting a conversation. Then move it up a notch, start creating connections with new people just for practice. I know it's hard. But another thing to do is also put the affirmations on your phone of what you want to accomplish. "I have the courage to approach anybody, I have the courage to start a conversation." And then start doing things when you are out such as smiling, be friendly, be open in your body language, and that will also leave room for you to be approached.

"What affirmation should I use?"

Well, it really is based on what you want to accomplish. Do you want to accomplish becoming more confident? Do you want to accomplish better communication? Do you want to accomplish better body language? What does that look like to you? Take a minute and write down five things that you want to accomplish and then turn those into affirmations.

"How much is too much?"

I think there's a balance between being needy and over the top and just having that ease. You can approach someone with a basic conversation but know when to stop if they feel suffocated. Watch someone's body language to know when to leave them alone. You don't want to follow someone the whole night, make the connection, then go hang out with your friends again. A little trick, when you're talking to someone, turn your body slightly away from them so they feel like they can leave the conversation. Now, if you're on a date, that's different, you're there for that reason, but I'm talking about someone you just met, you don't want them to feel like they can't get away from you. When you create more openness, to allow that freedom, that's when you become more attractive. However, on a first date, if you're attracted to them, you are turned to them. Remember the belly button rule, your belly button is turned towards them. Don't be overly needy and I wouldn't ask for their phone number right away. I wouldn't want to keep approaching them throughout the night, I would let the man take the lead. There are times where I think you can give your number out, but just be careful with that. You want to create a little connection and you want them to pursue you. So if you pursue too much, people run in the wrong direction. However, if you're about to leave and you had a great connection with someone, write your number down, slip it to them as you say "I'd love to continue our conversation" and then walk away.

"How do I stop getting anxious when they don't answer?"

When they don't answer their phone or messages. That's another important experience to practice letting go and letting it be easy. You text someone and they don't respond, let it go. There's nothing worse than someone who keeps texting you looking for a response when you don't answer. People have things going on. People are busy, like when I'm working, I don't text people back, even if it's my best friend. When I'm in my zone of working, I don't want to be bothered. And I don't answer my husband immediately all the time. He doesn't always answer me immediately either. He has a job that's very demanding. And if I text him, I don't expect a response right back. And we have both always been like that, and it's been great. Because he knows how busy I am. I know how busy he is. So we don't freak out. We respect each other's space. So if someone doesn't respond right away, it's no big deal. People have lives, they're busy. Don't worry about it. Now, if somebody doesn't respond for days, then they're simply not into you, and that's okay. They're simply not your person. When they don't respond, don't get worried about it. If someone doesn't communicate with you in a timely fashion, then why would you want to be in a relationship with them anyway? Because that shows what will happen in the future. You want someone who communicates well. Communication is key in a long-term healthy relationship. Another thing is, if you're waiting for somebody to text you back and keep checking your phone you're giving off the energy of neediness. For example your mind is racing with the thoughts of, " I want to text him to text me back. I keep checking my phone. Where is he? Is he on Facebook? He is online, but he hasn't text me." That energy is so crazy. It just gets you all worked up, I've done it, we've all done it, but it puts out that needy energy. That is something we want to stay away from. One of the key things in flirting is openness, not needy, clingy energy. So if you text somebody and they're not texting you back, put your phone somewhere else and go do something that takes your mind off of that text message or that person. Go out with your friends, go out on another date if you're not exclusive, put your mind off of that person. Because people fill our energy too much sometimes. And when you have a needy energy with someone, they can feel it. However, when we let go, it is like clockwork that we get a response. Have you noticed, for example when you're over a guy and you're dating someone else or having fun and enjoying your life and you're no longer focused on your ex, they call out of the blue. The energy you put off when you're free, flowing and enjoying life is an attraction magnet. But when you're needy and clingy and you're waiting for that text message or waiting for that response, that person can feel it. It's best just to let that message go and go do your thing.

Here's the point I want to end with.

What is your ultimate goal? Is it to find your soulmate? How is your future self acting? What is the highest version of yourself doing, saying? Where is she? What type of person is she with? Let's say you already have your soulmate. You're in an amazing relationship. How is your future self feeling? Is it peace, love, a life of fun, happiness? Think about how your future self is feeling at that moment. You're confident and at ease, become that, embody it. Because what we feel and what we focus on is what we manifest. Think about that. How is your future self already feeling in that place of where you want to be? And be in that place now. Because when we go into that place and we start having those feelings and envisioning that future, we are already putting ourselves into that place. That's how we manifest our soulmates, and that's a whole other topic, but I just want to leave you with that. So when you walk into a room, you're already feeling those feelings. You already own the place. You're taking the steps to start the journey of creating the life of your dreams with your future partner.

Remember to get someone's attention and raise your attraction level on a date.

1. Show your confidence and happiness within yourself.
2. Highlight your passions
3. Show you're human. You're authentic.
4. Don't treat the date like an interview. Treat it like a comfortable, fun conversation with a friend.

I believe in you and the ability to create a life beyond your wildest dreams. You are worthy of more love and being in a healthy flourishing relationship. This is your official permission slip to step into the highest version of yourself, get out there and go find the man of your dreams.

XO

Amanda Rose